A Suitcase Full of Stories

PEDAGOGICAL DOCUMENTATION FOR EARLY EDUCATION

Avril McMonagle

978-1915502-59-9

All rights reserved

Copyright © Avril McMonagle 2024
Cover design: 2funkidesign.com

Avril McMonagle has asserted her moral right to be identified as the author of this work. The material in this publication is protected by copyright law. Except as may be permitted by law, no part of the material may be reproduced or transmitted in any form or by any means, adapted, or lent without the written permission of the copyright owner. Published in Ireland by Orla Kelly Publishing.

Orla Kelly Publishing
27 Kilbrody
Mount Oval
Rochestown
Cork
Ireland

This book is dedicated to educators everywhere who allow education of the mind to play second fiddle to education of the heart.

About the Book

A Suitcase Full of Stories is a must-read for any early childhood educator or organisation dedicated to providing young children with the best learning experiences. Written by Avril McMonagle, with 30 years of experience in early childhood care and education, you will come away with a fresh and innovative perspective on documentation, rather than just seeing it as an administrative task.

You will also better understand the Learning Story Approach and Emergent Curriculum Planning and through real-life examples, see how using digital documentation can enhance your teaching and provide a rich learning experience for children.

Prepare for your pedagogical practices to be enhanced through pedagogical documentation techniques, insights and strategies to help create a more inclusive and engaging learning environment for young children.

Here is a taster of what is covered:

- How early childhood educators contribute to each child's life story.

- The power of Pedagogical documentation through stories as a potent tool for listening, analysing, progressing, and revisiting children's learning.

- The significance of using stories to build emotional connection, and make learning experiences personally relevant and memorable for children.

- The importance of validating children by acknowledging, valuing, and being part of their stories.

- Adapting components from different educational approaches to create vibrant and meaningful learning experiences is necessary.

- An introduction to the MOSAIC Educator, digital documentation system capturing the progression of learning and responses through a child-inspired, strength-based adaptation of the Learning Story approach.

- An overview of multi-modal documentation, which incorporates multiple perspectives and voices in the documentation process, including children and their families.

- Learning story examples created on the MOSAIC Educator application are included throughout the book, providing practical insights and understanding.

- Key messages emphasising the importance of a balanced invisible suitcase in early childhood education, recognising individual strengths, preferences, and interests, positively impacting documentation practices.

About the Author

Avril McMonagle has dedicated her working life to early childhood education and possesses a diverse skills-set consisting of practical, academic, management and policy expertise accumulated over the past 30 years. Being at the forefront of a range of pioneering initiatives to enhance quality standards in early education nationally and internationally; the legacy of her work is well evidenced.

Avril established her own business MOSAIC Digital Solutions for Early Education Ltd in 2019. The company flagship product is the MOSAIC Educator Pedagogical Documentation System – a digital application used by Educators to support a unique learning pathway for every child.

www.mosaicearlyed.com

Foreword

Professor Rosie Flewitt

Stories are the way that children spin webs of meaning into their lives. Through stories, children connect with and join the complexity of the social and cultural worlds in which they are born.

This book, which is written in a highly engaging and accessible manner, offers an antidote for early educators, for parents and for young children. The chapters present clear, helpful and practicable examples of how educators might support children to document their own learning journeys through storytelling and pedagogical documentation, including the opportunities available in the MOSAIC digital documentation app, which is based on principles of attending to children's perspectives long since celebrated by Alison Clark and Peter Moss in the UK (Clark and Moss 2001, 2005; Clark 2017) and by Margaret Carr in New Zealand (2001).

McMonagle also speaks to the challenges of documenting children's learning - the time it takes, the constant enthusiasm required, the need for training and the collective support that is essential to sustain imaginative approaches to documenting young children's learning. The documentation practices advocated in this book validate and celebrate educators' largely unrecognised practices in the classroom - listening, observing taking notes and reflecting critically and constructively on the busy comings and goings of children's lives and learning.

In this book, McMonagle foregrounds the place of imagination, creativity, play and stories in the early years classroom. These are the glue that hold learning together.

Introduction
A story about stories

Childhood is never truly confined to the past. It is a story that is inwardly recalled again and again.

Childhood is the first, and most important chapter, that makes up the multi-layered story of our lives. For those of us who work in the field of early childhood care and education, we have a collective responsibility to ensure each child's story is as constructive to life outcomes as is achievable.

Through this book, I aim to show that pedagogical documentation through stories is a powerful mechanism for **listening-in, analysing, progressing** and **revisiting children's story of learning**. This makes documentation a formidable pedagogical tool for early education.

How is this possible?

The answer is that stories create a context or environment that allows us to remember.

For babies, toddlers and young children, when learning experiences are based on things already familiar to them, they are stored in the mind and imagination as **a story**. This enables children to organise, imagine, understand, recall. And, above all, learn.

I frequently use the terms **'meaningful'** and **'lived experience'**. This is intentional.

When a story approach is used to document children's learning, the story is packed with familiar characters, people, peers, places and things. This is the child's **lived context and environment which acts as a springboard for learning**.

Stories also have the power to connect with others and move us emotionally. This is particularly true of young children's stories. Data and facts may convince someone intellectually, but stories will **evoke emotion**.

When stories are emotionally persuasive, they engage us on a deeper level, making them more effective and **embedded in memory**.

There is no more important validation that we can relay to children than – **'I value your story, I want to see and hear your story, I want to be part of your story'**.

This means that stories are the oldest form of education that we know.

Preface
My story and the story of MOSAIC

For me, early childhood education has been a lifelong interest, passion and career. My belief in the power of meaningful early education for life outcomes has never faltered.

Over the years, I have worked in early education from a variety of perspectives - as an educator, a lecturer, a company manager, an advisor, a mentor, a policy writer, a researcher and an author. Each role has given me solid grounding, perspective and understanding of early education from differing viewpoints. **These collective experiences have shaped my story.**

Now, within the creative scope of my own business, my continued passion for the **early childhood story** is my motivation to continue. I am guided by a clear mission statement – *'it is easier to build strong children than repair broken adults'* and this ethos is central to all the work and products provided by my business.

A special interest

Every professional educator has a specific interest in a particular area of early education. For me, this is the **fundamental importance of emotional well-being for learning supported by seeing the child as an individual**.

When working with young children as an educator, I vividly remember seeing the difference that meaningful, child-led experiences can make to children's learning and more importantly, how they feel about themselves. This was the beginning of a career-long special interest in the importance of **'listening-in'** to every child to discover their unique strengths and interests as a way of supporting well-being, learning and development.

Major influences to my work and thinking over the years include the critical nature of emotional intelligence to children's life outcomes (Goleman, 1995), the Learning Story Approach (Carr, 2001); the Mosaic Approach to listening, pedagogy and research (Clark, 2017), and the Reggio Emilia Approach to documentation (Malaguzzi, 1996).

Taking learning from each approach and applying the components to suit early childhood practice in a particular context is the key to creating vibrant and meaningful learning experiences for babies, toddlers and young children. I have never been an advocate of a one size fits all approach to early childhood curriculum. I favour thematic frameworks like Aistear (2009) and Te Whāriki (1996, 2017) as they allow scope for the **creativity of the proficient educator** to provide meaningful, child-inspired experiences.

As I have moved from role to role in my professional life, I have studied and practiced assessment methods, authored publications and articles, developed and delivered training programmes. Furthermore, I've been a tireless advocate for the Learning Story method of assessment for learning.

Whilst I have observed some wonderful practice over the years, I struggle to accept the mixed messages coming from training, policy, support services and inspection bodies about what constitutes meaningful, **child-inspired documentation.**

This has contributed to confusion among educators, which can lead to inconsistent or ineffective practice, not to mention general frustration. This is not good for children. The practical explanations and examples within this book will help clear the fog.

Step forward MOSAIC Educator

An important milestone on my business roadmap was the development of a **digital documentation instrument for educators** that would enable professional documentation.

Having previously written and designed a training programme and materials on the learning story approach 10 years earlier (Building Pictures of Learning, 2009), I wanted to take the learning from the passage of time and merge this with the unique possibilities provided by digital documentation.

Choosing the name was easy.

The little owl is symbolic for me. Not only does it represent a MOSAIC, it represents a collective of experiences, learning, people, breakages and opportunities that have made up my career in early education. A little mosaic patterned owl denotes wisdom, education and pieces to make the whole. It represents my story of learning.

In the first year of business, the pilot versions of **'MOSAIC Educator'** and **'MOSAIC Family'** digital apps went live. I was unprepared for the absolute incredulity of seeing the little MOSAIC owl on the App stores – to see the idea come to fruition – especially as a solo project by a new business. I don't want to understate the testing journey, money, isolation and stress to get to that point. But I have always been able to call tenacity my friend!

MOSAIC - A documentation system designed for children

When designing MOSAIC, several essential pre-requisites were identified to shape the design and functionality of the digital documentation system.

Inclusive, adaptable and accessible

Of importance was to create a documentation system that was **inclusive for all children, early childhood services, educators and families**. MOSAIC is not curtailed by a child's age, ability, home language, traits or characteristics.

It is a system based on children's unique strengths to ensure that no child is disadvantaged by the documentation process.

The participation and privacy rights of the child

Led by the ethos of children's rights, the MOSAIC documentation system provides the space for children to **participate** in the documentation process itself. Child voice can be captured in multiple ways across the system. The **child's right to privacy** also underpins design where each child has their own e-storybook (e-portfolio) linked to nominated family members only.

Learning process and response

Being able to capture **progression in learning** is facilitated through a visible connection between the planning section of learning stories, emergent curriculum plans and transition reporting. Child interests and needs are also a component of the emergent planning system on MOSAIC.

Child-inspired, strength-based

The child-inspired adaptation of the Learning Story approach which focuses on **child strengths**, ensures that children are not viewed or judged through a linear lens that focuses on school readiness and accountability. The variety of learning story perspectives and formats available allow the educator to balance curriculum goal focus, process focus and voice focus or a blend of all three.

Multiple perspectives and voices

It was important that MOSAIC incorporated **multiple voices** in the documentation process- most importantly the participation and voices of children themselves. MOSAIC has the capacity to involve and connect not only parents but the wider family, including those living in different parts of the world.

Multi-modal Stories

MOSAIC's multi-modality can capture children's diverse and subtle indications of learning - not just a physical collection of drawings and paintings. Educators can capture things that can go unnoticed - a facial expression, a gesture, a smile or a few words.

Overall MOSAIC Educator has lived up to its name not only in capturing all the components to present a vibrant picture of the **child's lived story** and the process of learning. The system draws on best practice from a range of pedagogical and research approaches for early education. This makes MOSAIC a storybook that captures **stories not only about children, but also for children and by children.**

> As you navigate this book, you will see learning story examples peppered throughout. Some stories have been borrowed from MOSAIC users with permission and child consent where appropriate. Others have been recreated to protect child privacy.
>
> You will see documented stories that bring the narrative to life and to a place of practical understanding and transference to practice.

Images

A huge thank you to members of *TribeMOSAIC from the following early childhood settings that answered the call to provide some of the images and stories that bring this book to life:

- Blossom Academy Pre-School, Greencastle, Co. Donegal
- Clare's Little Stars, Ballybofey, Co. Donegal
- Fairytales Daycare, Milford and Rathmullan, Co. Donegal
- Laugh and Learn Childcare, Quigley's Point, Co. Donegal
- Learn n Play Pre-School, Letterkenny, Co. Donegal
- Little Stars Pre-School and Afterschool, Moville, Co. Donegal.

Permission granted
- Additional images:
    - Stock photography licensed from Shutterstock, Adobe Stock and Canva.
    - Personal collection with permission.

Children's real names are not used.
Early childhood setting identities not disclosed where images feature children.

*TribeMOSAIC: A collective term used for early childhood settings that use the MOSAIC Documentation System.

Contents

INTRODUCTION vii
A Story about Stories
The oldest form of education that we know.

PREFACE.. ix
My Story and the story of MOSAIC
My personal journey in early education and of developing the MOSAIC Multi-modal documentation system.

CHAPTER 1 1
The Invisible Suitcase
The fundamental role of emotional intelligence for learning including positive dispositions to learn and the role of documentation in seeing and validating the individual child.

CHAPTER 2 24
Enabling the Enablers
The role of the proficient educator and the supports needed for professional documentation practice.

CHAPTER 3 36
Documentation isn't an Optional Extra
Understanding the functions of documentation and why it is central to child-inspired learning.

CHAPTER 4 56
What's the Story?
The Learning Story Approach and why it is uniquely positioned as an effective method of assessment for learning in early education.

CHAPTER 5 70
The Voice Box
Writing perspectives and techniques to increase the visibility of child voice in the documentation process.

CHAPTER 6 91
A collection of stories
Learning story formats and examples for babies, toddlers and young children.

CHAPTER 7 110
Pulling out the positives
Recognising individual strengths, preferences and interests and reflecting these in the documentation process.

CHAPTER 8 126
Revisit, recall, reimagine
Engaging children and parents as a means of connecting and involving all stakeholders in the documentation process.

CHAPTER 9 147
Why predict the unpredictable?
How ongoing documentation informs emergent curriculum planning and the provision of child inspired learning experiences.

CHAPTER 10 179
Packing the Suitcase
A summary of key messages for a balanced invisible suitcase.

CHAPTER 1
The Invisible Suitcase

A STORY OF LEARNING
I encountered multiple teachers throughout my education. Not one of them could see me. My strengths and talents were masked by an introverted nature, fear of authority and quiet personality. Over the years, their misplaced judgements contributed to a lifetime of low self-esteem, perfectionism, overworking and imposter syndrome. Today, as educators, we can do better.

As the starting point for documentation, this chapter highlights the importance of 'seeing' each child as an individual. It also highlights the fundamental role of emotional intelligence in finding the security to learn. And, the impact of all interactions and relationships in early childhood on the child's lifelong self-image is explained and portrayed through the notion of
'The Invisible Suitcase'.

The Invisible Suitcase

'I carry an invisible suitcase filled with experiences, encounters and messages. Some are positive, some are negative and some are buried for later.

You will never see the suitcase. But it is there.
The contents accumulate during my childhood, slowly building an emotional toolkit for life. Some content will propel me forward. Some will limit and separate me from my potential. And some will trigger a response when I least expect it.

Be aware of my suitcase; what is already in it and what you can add. Listen-in, see me, value my unique contribution and respond to me.

Fill my invisible suitcase with positive messaging, love, connection and belonging. Work to balance my suitcase, particularly when it is out of balance. The suitcase will carry my story.'

Filling the Suitcase

Self-esteem has been largely forged within the family by the time a child starts school. This makes the early education experience instrumental in nurturing positive dispositions for lifelong emotional well being.

As a child navigates life, they carry an invisible suitcase. It will accompany the child through adolescence and into adulthood. The contents of this suitcase are the totality of the child's experiences, relationships and interactions accumulated over the years. Not everything will be re constructive, and some can be downright damaging.

The invisible suitcase fulfils the role of an **ever-present inner voice**. One full of messages, learned behaviours and image of self. Some of the messages accumulated have the potential to propel the child forward in every aspect of well being and development. Some will limit the child and separate them from their **actual worth and potential**. Some will function as unwelcome triggers and emotional barriers well into adulthood.

Storing positive messaging

Children come to early childhood settings with vastly different life experience. Some come from homes where parents and family members provide a secure loving environment, rich in love, emotional security and interaction.

On the other hand, some children come from an environment where homelessness, domestic violence, drug or alcohol dependency, neglect or adverse parenting is part of everyday life.

It is vital that all children **accumulate a bank of positive messaging** to store in their invisible suitcase.

This is essential to build the strong mental toolkit needed to navigate life.

For children with supportive life experiences, the continued nurturing of stable relationships outside the home, will **reinforce the positive messaging** contained in their suitcase. For children coming from adverse environments, meaningful interactions from a key person in the early childhood setting will dilute negative experiences and store alternative messaging in the invisible suitcase. This will go a long way in supporting healthy emotional well being.

Actual worth and self-esteem

We are unique from birth. As a tiny newborn baby, we possess vast intellectual potential and power. **This is our actual worth.**

No one can alter this blueprint. It is always there.

Conversely, for the child who suffers emotional trauma, this can lead to a **distortion of all core emotional states**, becoming integrated into the developing sense of self.

In response to this, the child employs a number of coping strategies in order to protect their real self. This is no less a strategy for survival to function in an unsafe environment.

For many children, actual worth, or potential, gradually becomes eroded – mainly as a protection mechanism from not being valued, heard or loved. The layers of the erosion can start to build in early childhood.

The result shapes the level of self-esteem, for example, self-confidence, identity, feeling of belonging, and feeling competent. These collective factors are central to the child's ability to learn and progress.

Finding the security to learn

Intelligence is a highly sought-after characteristic.

However, intelligence should not be pigeon-holed into the ability to solve complex mathematical problems or achieve high marks in education. There are many types of intelligence, spanning a range of important qualities and skills. And one of the most important of these is **emotional intelligence**.

The security to learn is paramount to the *ability* to learn.

Several factors contribute to the capacity of babies, toddlers and young children to develop communicative, cognitive and regulative abilities. To name a few, this includes family circumstances, stress levels, and neurodiversity. Taking any number of circumstantial variables into consideration, the need to nurture emotional intelligence in early childhood is not only obvious, but essential.

> *Whilst a child may not have the power to change life circumstances, supportive relationships and a variety of positive pedagogical strategies will go a long way in affording them the emotional security to thrive and learn. This brings the role of the proficient educator to the centre of early education.*

Emotional Intelligence

Emotional intelligence refers to having the skills and ability to **understand, utilise and manage our own feelings**.

It also includes the capacity to understand and respond to the feelings of others.

This type of intelligence isn't measured by IQ tests, yet it's crucial to help us work through challenges and respond to situations successfully. It also helps us make positive connections with the people around us.

For educators, nurturing emotional intelligence relates to supporting children to be psychologically aware and socially strong as a core component of child well being.

Understanding how to develop these dispositions and skills in children, and the lifelong benefits that can be derived from the, can have a huge impact on the effectiveness of learning experiences delivered in the early childhood setting.

The question should not be about the quality of early childhood education, but about the effectiveness of the early childhood curriculum in meeting the needs of the individual child.

Understanding emotional intelligence

The first to introduce the concept of multiple intelligences theory was psychologist Howard Gardner in the 1980s.

This theory proposes that there are multiple intelligences that we as humans can develop. Intrapersonal intelligence (understanding the self) and interpersonal intelligence (understanding others) are two of Gardner's intelligence types that make up the more general concept of emotional intelligence.

The psychologist Daniel Goleman (1995), described emotional intelligence as has having five basic parts:
- **Self-awareness:** Know feelings at a particular time and understand how moods affect others.
- **Self-regulation:** Control response to emotions. Consider possible consequences before acting.
- **Motivation:** Accomplish goals in spite of negative or distracting feelings.
- **Empathy:** Understand how others feel.
- **Social skills:** Manage relationships. Know what kind of behaviours get a positive response.

The benefits of Emotional Intelligence

Emotional intelligence has powerful benefits for mental well being. It is essential that these skills and dispositions are nurtured from early childhood.

A child who can self-regulate when they feel angry, is likely to do well in difficult circumstances. Likewise, a child who can understand and express their emotions, is likely to maintain healthier relationships than a child who screams or says inappropriate things when angry.

Consider two common scenarios. A child gets frustrated when they cannot complete a task. This could be a puzzle or climbing an obstacle. Instead of giving up, screaming in a temper, or throwing the object away, the child has learned the strategy to ask for help. Or an adult friend cancels a scheduled social meet-up as they got upsetting news. Instead of taking this personally and feeling rejected, you understand and make other plans. These responses may not seem all that significant. But they are **indicators of emotional intelligence**.

Emotional intelligence is also one of the positive characteristics that makes a proficient educator stand out. A sound understanding of feelings and the feelings of others, helps self-regulate emotions and can promote positivity and motivation. Learning to navigate patterns of thought and behaviour is essential for effective communication and relationship-building. Both with children and as part of an educator team. This also helps educators recognise and document children's emotional development as demonstrated in the story shown.

Created on MOSAIC Educator, May's story 'For Granda', reveals a lot about her emotional capabilities. Through the medium of her chalk drawing on the cement, May exhibits dispositions such as empathy, compassion and kindness. She associates 'love hearts' and flowers as something that will make her Granda feel 'happy and better'.

May is also aware of the meaningful use of technology and how she can use this to her advantage to communicate her ideas, thoughts and feelings. This documented story has made multiple connections possible and the emotional return will be meaningful to everyone involved.

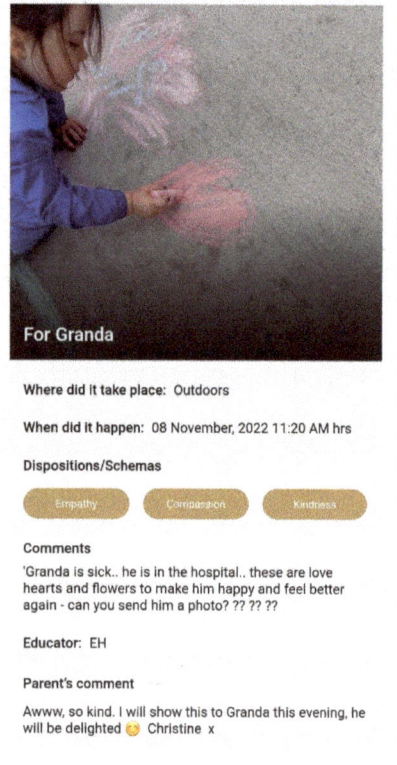

Positive Dispositions to Learn

Closely linked to emotional intelligence, the idea of dispositions has emerged as important in the debate about what is of lasting value in early learning. Learning dispositions can be thought of as characteristics or attitudes to learning we need for a successful and happy life.

When learning opportunities and engagement with others gives attention to the development of positive dispositions, a solid emotional foundation for all future well being, skills and knowledge-based learning is formed. Some positive dispositions for learning and for life are highlighted below.

Curiosity – natural state of inquisitiveness and desire to find out more.

Empathy – the ability to understand how another feels.

Cooperation – the ability to work with peers towards common goals.

Confidence – the belief in one's own abilities to learn and know.

Creativity – the ability to able to express oneself in different ways.

Independence – ability to do things for oneself.

Enthusiasm – the feeling of motivation.

Persistence – continuing to do or to try to do something that is difficult.

Imagination – the ability to mentally visualise new and different possibilities and scenarios.

Resilience – the ability to recover from experienced difficulty.

All learning is interconnected

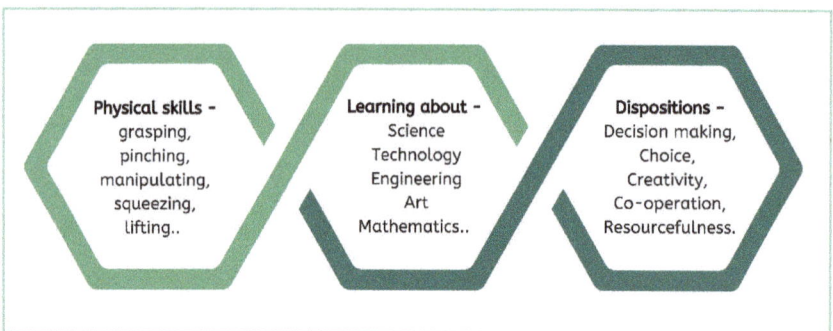

Dispositions develop alongside and in conjunction with children's acquisition of knowledge, skills, attitudes and understanding. For example, a group of children constructing with loose parts are developing a range of **manipulative abilities and physical skills** as well as learning about **science, technology, engineering, art and mathematics**. At the same time, these children are **developing positive dispositions** as they engage, plan and solve problems during their play.

Learning dispositions can also help children develop the **ability to deal with failure and change**. A failed attempt at challenging obstacles , with sensitive intervention by the educator, will nurture dispositions of self-confidence, perseverance and resilience. Children need to experience failure and not be overly protected from it. Encouraging a child to persist with difficulty, to use thinking questions, or to try again, demonstrates that one doesn't always succeed the first time. This experience shows the child that they may have to try again and again to achieve a goal. **These experiences foster resilience based on experience, feeling and understanding.**

Children who have successfully developed positive dispositions have conquered the most fundamental component of learning for life. Fundamentally, **they have learned how to learn**. The opposite is also true.

Seeing the individual child through documentation

Young children's self-esteem is based largely on their perceptions of how the important adults in their life interact with and respond to them.

This makes child-centred documentation an essential pedagogical strategy to enable the educator to **listen-in to the individual child and see their strengths, lived experience and personality**.

As learning stories capture a socially constructed story of learning in the context of **when, where, how and with whom** the learning took place, they are an effective way of capturing who the child is as a learner. Furthermore, learning stories note the things that motivate the child and their disposition to learn.

The extent to which children believe they have the characteristics valued by the important adults and peers in their lives features greatly in the development of **self-esteem and self-image**. This is especially true for children who are neurodiverse. It is important to support children to **see the strengths within their neurodiversity**. Children who display neurodiverse characteristics can feel more confidence and self-worth when they are recognised for their abilities, instead of their difference.

A useful way of engaging children to find out how they see themselves as learners is through **self-reflection**. How children describe their work, experiences and friendships will reveal their self-image and dispositions.

Educators take time to reflect with children about various learning experiences, creativity and interactions captured in their MOSAIC storybook.

This not only provides important **connective** experiences between the educator and children, but it also strengthens **positive emotional dispositions in the invisible suitcase**.

For example, the child will develop **self-esteem**, feel that their **work is valued**, improve **connections** with family, and see themselves as **participative learners** able to make choices and decisions.

There are five key building blocks to be mindful of when observing and responding to children's emotional abilities as part of the documentation process.

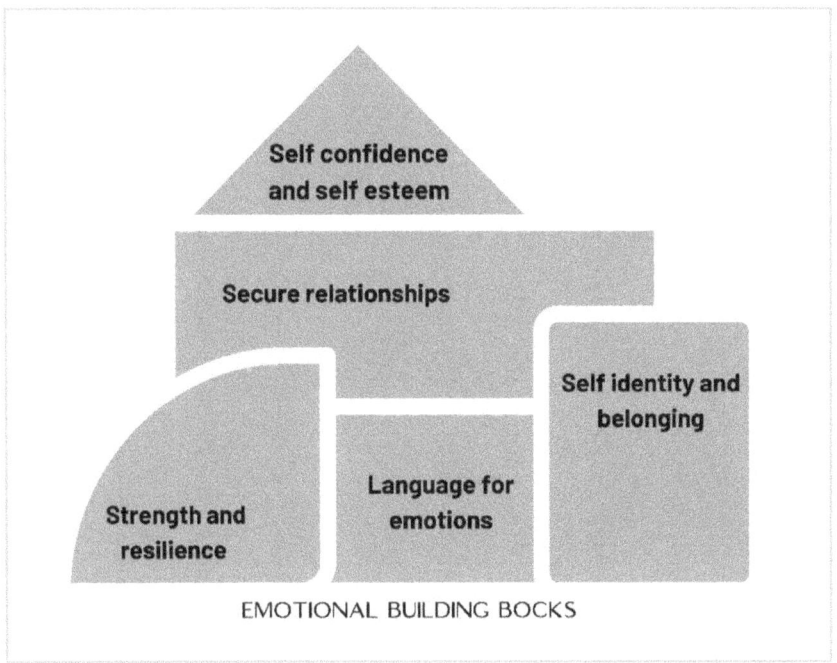

EMOTIONAL BUILDING BOCKS

1. **Identity and belonging**

    A child's self-identity is how they see their unique place in the world and the roles they have within their family, school and community.

    It is important that children develop a positive sense of their **own identity**, and they feel valued and respected as a unique individual.

    This contributes to children's understanding of themselves, relationships with others, self-esteem and self-belief. This is particularly important for children who are neurodiverse or exhibit multi-modal forms of communication, especially as they may be more vulnerable to being excluded.

The Documentation Response: Learning Stories should be based on the individual **interests, preferences, abilities and needs** of children.

2. **A language for emotions and feelings**
   It is important that adults help children recognise and understand different feelings and emotions by providing them with words and language to communicate how they feel. Children's understanding of their emotions contribute , not only to their understanding of themselves, but also to an understanding and awareness of the emotions of those around them.

   The Documentation Response: A child-inspired curriculum plan that provides for the development of descriptive emotional language and vocabulary.

3. **Inner strength and resilience**
   Inner strength and resilience refer to the ability to cope with the changes, challenges and adversities of life. For example, it could include a subtle adaptation such as an unexpected change to the daily routine to something bigger such as moving house or the arrival of a new baby. Essentially, this is nurturing a child's inner strength provides them with skills to be able to cope and deal with the unpredictable. It enables children to adapt and move forward in life.

   The Documentation Response: Listening-in, responding and planning for needs based experiences.

4. **Secure relationships**

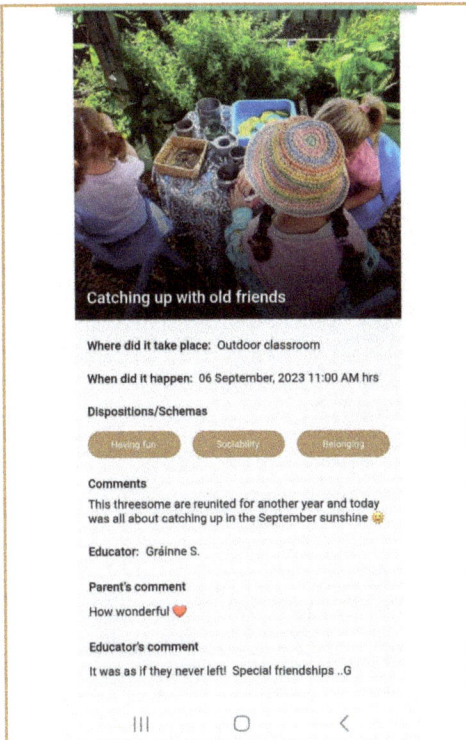

The most important aspect of any relationship for children, especially babies and toddlers, is that of a secure relationship. Within the safety of secure relationships, children can explore the world around them and be confident that if anything happens, they can rely on the adult to be there, to help them and make them feel safe.

The Documentation Response: Nurture interactions and engagement with others and scaffold relationship building.

5. **Self-confidence and self-esteem**

Self-esteem is our personal perception of ourselves. It is the knowledge that we are lovable, capable and unique. Good self-esteem in children means that they have established a sense of identity, self-worth and confidence in themselves and their abilities.

The Documentation Response: Validating interaction techniques and strategies both spontaneous and planned.

Supporting emotional intelligence in children

Practical engagement strategies for educators
Early childhood educators can play a crucial role in developing healthy emotional intelligence as part of the early childhood curriculum. Below are practical pedagogical strategies that can be used as part of everyday interactions and communications.

1. Validate feelings and show empathy
When a child is upset, validate their feelings and show empathy- *'I feel upset when I don't get to do what I want too'* or *'It is hard sometimes to keep working when I don't want to'*.

When a child sees that you understand how they're feeling on the inside, they'll feel less compelled to show you how they're feeling through unwanted behaviour.

2. Label Emotions
Support children to identify the emotion and recognise how they are feeling. Labelling **emotions as part of everyday interactions** expands children's emotional vocabulary. Furthermore, identifying emotions is also useful for learning to read other people and what they might be feeling.

When a child is upset, they lost a game or have to share a toy, you can say, *'It looks like you feel really angry right now. Is that right?'* If they look sad, you might say, *'Are you feeling disappointed that …?'*.

Emotional words such as angry, upset, worried and painful can all build a vocabulary to express feelings. Don't forget to share the words for positive emotions, too, such as happy, excited, thrilled or funny. Simple activities like showing children images of faces and helping them to identify the feelings the person might be having can be useful to build this skill.

3. Nurture Coping Skills

Once children recognise their emotions, they need to learn how to deal with those emotions in a healthy way. Knowing simple strategies to **calm themselves down, cheer themselves up or face their fears** are valuable.

Teach specific skills. For example, children may benefit from learning how to take a few deep breaths when they're angry to calm their body down. A simple one to utilise is deep breathing and **mindfulness** techniques.

Educators should be aware of different **calm down strategies that work best for a child**. This could be **a comfort object, a quiet space, music, physical exercise, a 'calm down kit' or sensory snacks**. Sensory snacks are 'go-to' snacks that provide oral sensory input and movement action. For example, cut up carrots or rice cakes to crunch loudly.

Building a 'Calm Down Kit' can help them to restore a sense of calm. A favourite creative activity, music, or lotions that smell nice are a few items that can help engage a child's senses and calm their emotions. Put the items in a special box that they decorate. Then, when they're upset, remind them to go get their calm down kit and practice using their tools to manage their emotions.

Stories, songs and creative role play are also valuable teaching activities to nurture and explore emotional learning.

KNOW A CHILD'S PREFERRED CALM DOWN STRATEGY

Hug a friend, Cuddle a weighted blanket or pillow.

Listen to music; Stress ball; Fidget toy; Book.

Blow bubbles; Count breaths; Blow a pinwheel, Blow up a balloon.

Bounce/Swing; Run/Dance; Ride a bicycle; Bounce a ball.

Water/Sand/dough; Personal toy/blanket; Chewy snack; Paint.

EMOTIONAL WELL-BEING
SUPPORTING CHILDREN TO SELF-REGULATE USING THEIR PREFERRED CALMING STRATEGY

4. Talk about challenges and develop problem-solving skills

A core part of building emotional intelligence involves learning how to **solve problems**. Don't brush over problems when they arise. Use them as a learning opportunity.

Support children to identify at least three ways they might solve this problem. Solutions don't have to be good ideas. Initially, the goal is to just brainstorm ideas.

Once they've identified at least three possible solutions, support the child to choose the **best or most achievable option**. When a child makes mistakes, work through what could have been done differently. Eventually this will lead to the ability to solve problems effectively by themselves.

5. Be an effective role model

Emotional intelligence isn't only important for children.

For educators, focusing on self-emotional intelligence is vital in the demanding role of an educator . The best way to teach children how to express feelings is by actively **modelling appropriate language, skills and dispositions**. Self-reflection techniques and reflective practice support this.

Use feeling words in your everyday conversation and practice talking about them. Say things like, *'I feel angry when I see ….'*, or *'I feel happy when…'*.

Being a role-model for appropriate and positive behaviours support children to develop dispositions as highlighted in the graphic on the next page.

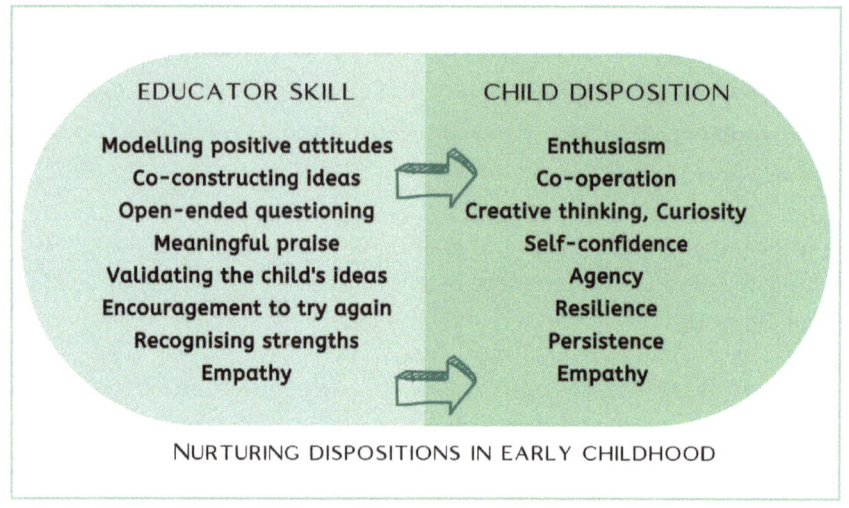

NURTURING DISPOSITIONS IN EARLY CHILDHOOD

6. Listen-in, be positive and be responsive.

This is characterised by:

- Maintaining eye contact – looking at children as you engage.
- Being attentive and present.
- Interacting on the child's level.
- Exaggerating facial expression.
- Demonstrating empathy.
- Being positive and receptive – showing excitement at children's attempts to communicate.
- Fostering friendship skills with peers – helping children make friends.
- Promoting cooperation – playing cooperation games and acknowledging positive behaviour.
- Using humour and having fun.

7. Listen to children and practice 'Serve and Return'.

This is characterised by:

- Making time to sensitively join in with play – following the child's lead and interest.
- Listening carefully and scaffolding new language – expanding and extending what the child says.
- Asking open ended questions – using gestures for younger children.
- Taking turns in conversations.
- Waiting - allowing the child time to listen, process and respond.

8. Seize opportunities to communicate during play and everyday activities.

This is characterised by:

- 1:1 time with a Key Person.
- Asking questions.
- Commenting on play activities.
- Expressing feelings.
- Using meaningful praise
- Commenting on books or pictures.
- Asking about preferred toys and activities.
- Inviting choice and decision making.
- Playing circle games and activities.
- Chatting or singing at snack time.
- Setting up a 'Chat Chair'.

Educators have the power to balance the invisible suitcase

One of the most privileged positions of the early childhood educator is to work to ensure that each child's suitcase is filled with positive messages and meaningful interactions.

There is no more important role than to add balance to a suitcase that starts its earliest life unbalanced.

Educators achieve this by building secure relationships and practicing affirming interactions. They pay attention to and listen-in to the child, see and hear their voice and respond to their needs. It is worth remembering that tone of voice, facial expression, levels of attentiveness and body posture communicate **subliminal messages** – either positive or negative, to the child.

Simple interactions like a genuine smile, good eye contact, a hug or stopping to hear what the child has to say will add positive messaging to the child's suitcase. These **affirming interactions** are at the core of effective early education and care.

Genuine, secure relationships and positive interactions demonstrate to the child that their voice and opinion are valued and important. Regardless of the child's home environment, this type of experience will build a bank of positive inner messaging that will be drawn on throughout the child's life.

This is a job worth doing. And worth doing well.

By nurturing emotional intelligence in children, we can help to shape a more caring, kind and thoughtful future.

Educators can support the development of children's emotional well-being and dispositions to learn, providing them with the tools to fly.

CHAPTER 2
Enabling the enablers

A STORY OF LEARNING

I think of educators as enablers. The way an educator interacts and responds to a child is the key determining factor for positive well-being and learning outcomes. The way an educator encourages a child to persist with difficulty, to use thinking questions, to pursue interests is the most impactful way to nurture positive dispositions to learn.

Characterising the role of the proficient educator is important. Just as necessary is characterising the attitude of the educator. Having worked with educators of varied experience, training and attitude over the years, the educators who are most responsive, and therefore effective, for children's learning, care and development are those who have enthusiasm, passion and energy for their role. The dedication, skill and proficiency of the early childhood educator deserves professional recognition, value and respect.

The challenges facing documentation

Documentation itself is not a challenge; **but there are challenges for effective documentation practice**. This is often alluded to as 'the demands of documentation', the 'challenges of documenting' or 'the lack of time for documenting'. Time will always be a factor in such a responsive role. However, an unenthusiastic attitude places documentation outside the curriculum, as an optional extra if educators can find the time. This is a noteworthy misrepresentation of this important engagement and learning support for babies, toddlers and young children.

Any function, including documentation, when not understood or valued for what it can offer children, becomes a chore. Training and experience, or access to continuing professional development, can vary greatly among educators. Some educators understand what documentation is, but may not have the practical experience to transfer theory to practice. Some have been taught multiple methods of observation, but have no idea how to use observations to analyse or scaffold learning. **A collective responsibility to get this right for children is vital.**

Educators as scaffolders

Contemporary learning theories, including constructivism, cognitive theory, and sociocultural theory, share core principles including that children co-construct knowledge, and that learning and development are socially supported processes. This makes the role and expertise of the educator a crucial component of this social construct.

Documentation is a good example of where learning theory is **practically applied** in everyday pedagogical practice. Take formative assessment and Vygotsky's (1978) model of scaffolding, for example. The zone of proximal development 'is the space between the actual developmental level as determined by independent problem solving and the level of potential development as determined through problem solving under adult guidance or in collaboration with more capable peers'. (1978, p. 86).

Using this model, where supportive others help move the learner forward by providing a scaffold, is essentially the same as the proficient educator using meaningful, child focussed observation and providing a suitable response to support learning. In other words, **the educator enables learning through timely engagement and response**.

Enabling the enablers

Educators come to their role with varied amounts of experience, training and expertise. This makes it important for the early childhood setting to have a consistent framework for documentation practice **embedded within the practice of the setting**.

Like any skill, documentation must be learned. It is not good enough to expect educators to have this skill without relevant support to learn the skill. Every early childhood setting should have a person acting as Pedagogical Leader. This person requires sound documentation experience and the ability to guide educators within the team. If this is not possible within a team, then pedagogical support should be sought externally.

Daniel's Tour and Map – 'Can you see my coat hanging up?'

The Story.. You took me on an interesting tour of our preschool today Daniel. We walked through the playroom, your favourite areas outside, the toilets and the kitchen. You chatted confidently as we carried out our tour and you were full of information. I asked if you would like to draw a map to put on the wall and you drew the most wonderfully creative map of our preschool.

Daniel' perspective.. 'This is my map of my school, I like maps .. this is outside, that's my favourite. Then this room here (playroom) that's me and Cian playing with the blocks. Here is the toilets and the kitchen – we are not allowed in the kitchen because its only for teachers. I like outside the best because I can climb on the ropes and play chase with Cian and Aine. Can you see my coat hanging up?'

What we know now to help you learn..
You have told me that your preferred place is outdoors, you can communicate your thoughts and ideas through drawing and reflection and has formed specific friendship bonds with Cian and Aine. You have a sense of space, perspective and belonging. Let's see what other maps we can find, draw and explore. And yes Daniel, I can clearly see your coat hanging up!

*As a new child joining the pre-school, the educator **understands** the importance of ensuring that Daniel is familiar and comfortable in his new environment. The educator **responds** by accompanying him on a tour and **extends** the activity by encouraging him to draw a picture which he calls a 'map'.*
*From **reflecting** on Daniel's actual commentary, the educator **evaluates** Daniel's interests, preferences and growing connections with others. The educator **documents** this succinctly through photography, child voice and narrative and will **use** the information to plan for **progression**. This story when shared with family, will be a springboard for lots of conversations to further support Daniel's transition to a new pre-school.*

A considerable bank of knowledge and expertise

Documentation begins with noticing and observing. However, knowing what to do with what has been **noticed and observed** is more complex than it sounds. Participative documentation requires the educator to have knowledge about the child, their lived experiences, interests and learning preferences.

In order to understand the child, the educator must have a solid foundation in child development and play as a means for learning for all children. They must also learn documentation techniques and writing skills . Educators must feel confident in their work and have professional development support when needed.

When educators look to the pedagogical documentation practice within the early childhood setting, below is some practical guidance as to what needs to be in place and questions to ask:

1. **Knowing the documentation practice of the early childhood setting.** Is there a curriculum statement and documentation policy in place? What format/system is used? Is documentation carried out by a Key Person ? When is documentation carried out? How are parents involved and what does this look like?

2. **Building personal dispositions to document.** Do you lack confidence to document information to share with others? Is there an option to build confidence by carrying out in class documentation first before sharing

information with parents? What continuing professional support on documentation is available to you?

3. **Develop literacy skills for narrative documentation.** Is this an area where you need support? Do you need to start with adding photo captions and develop confidence from there? Are spell check options available to you? Can you compile drafts first? Is someone available to proof read your work in the early days?

*On the next page, Alina's story, created on MOSAIC Educator, shows that the educator **recognises** that baby Alina is practicing a trajectory schema. She **captures the learning episode** using **Translated Voice speaking to Alina** and describing her play behaviour as observed. She **aligns the story** to the learning goals and dispositions achieved and **plans for progression** of Alina's interest in trajectory and how things move. Alina's learning preference is then **shared with family** and where the educator suggests sending on some further information to the parent on Schemas.*

Alina you are showing me through your play that you are interested in trajectory schema. I know this because you like playing with the yellow ball and rolling it across the floor. You watch intently as the ball rolls away from you and as soon as it stops, you roll into action! You are so agile when you quickly crawl after the ball, showing great preseverence to find it when it rolls under the chair.
I know you are proud of your achievements as you laugh and shout 'yeeah' when the ball is recovered - only to roll it again for a repeat rolling adventure around the babyroom floor.

1. I am discovering, exploring and refining my gross and fine motor skills.
2. I am demonstrating determination and perseverance.
3. I have my own interests and learning preferences.
4. I use a range of body movements, facial expressions, and early vocalisations such as babbling to show feelings and share information.

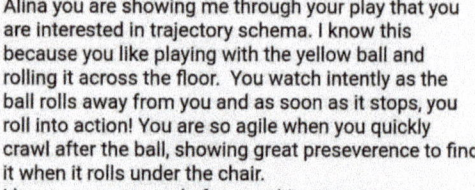

Dispositions/Schemas

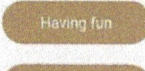

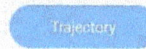

You can help me build on this by:
I am working out how I can make things move. I do this repeatedly through my play as I am testing out this idea. Give me lots different objects that roll - different weights, sizes and textures. Try rolling on a tabletop, outdoors and in water. Introduce describing words as we play, support my developing physical movement skills and praise my fantastic efforts.

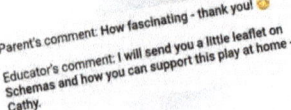

Parent's comment: How fascinating - thank you! 😊

Educator's comment: I will send you a little leaflet on Schemas and how you can support this play at home - Cathy.

Only when educators can draw upon particular skills and knowledge will they be able to effectively document and make informed decisions and plans. Sound documentation practice requires an interdependent blend of knowledge, skills, attitudes and support as outlined below.

Knowledge – Documentation of Learning is based on sound professional knowledge

- How children's rights apply to early education.
- Child development and neurodiversity.
- Play as a vehicle for learning.
- Schematic patterns in play.
- Socio-cultural learning theory.
- Ethical considerations.
- Multi-modal documentation and how it is used to support learning.

Skill – Documentation requires a specific skill set

- Active listening.
- Ability to tune-in to children regardless of mode of communication, ability or personality.
- Scaffolding and co-construction.
- Interaction, appropriate intervention and engagement skills.
- Organisation and decision making.
- Writing techniques and perspectives.
- Creative documentation techniques (e.g., living wall displays).
- Self-reflection and critique of practice.
- Analysis and planning.

Attributes – Documentation necessitates a positive mindset by the educator

- Positive communicator.
- Creative and energetic.
- Respectful of children and families including families who are culturally and linguistically diverse.
- Compassion and empathy.
- Flexible and open to professional development and upskilling.

Consideration for educator proficiency

When early childhood services require documentation practice to be carried out to a high standard, consideration must be given to the **support available for educators to do this**.

Educators straight from college, may have limited practical experience of real-life child documentation. They will need support to navigate and become familiar with the **full documentation system** used in the early childhood setting. This includes **documentation for care, documentation for learning and documentation to share information**. Educators moving from other early childhood settings may have been using a different system or have limited knowledge of the processes involved.

Good documentation requires not only the skill set required from the educator, but suitable tools, consideration and support from the early childhood setting.

In addition to educator proficiency, adequate time, mental energy and confidence are prerequisites for engagement with purposeful pedagogical documentation.

A framework for support

The early childhood setting should ensure that a range of enabling factors are in place if effective documentation practice is to be realised. This includes:

- Organisational buy-in.

- Professional development and capacity building.

- Systems and resources.

Organisational buy-in

Where early childhood settings are invested in good documentation practice, this is evident in the ethos and values of the service. Policies and procedures for documentation practice and parental engagement are in place and a children's rights approach is evident in both ethos and everyday practice.

The curriculum framework followed, and the underpinning principles of this framework will view babies, toddlers and young children as active, participative learners and advocate for time to enable children to lead their own learning experience. The early childhood setting should adopt a **consistent and systematic approach** to documentation, where all educators working within the setting have been given instruction, understand the process and are supported when needed.

Professional development and capacity building

Early childhood settings that have a proactive approach to the continuing professional development of educators will reach beyond recurring mandatory training programmes.

Whilst these are necessary, just as necessary are continuing professional development programmes on participative documentation techniques and skills, seeing and hearing the voice of the child and planning an emergent child-inspired curriculum. Educator support may be identified through support and supervision meetings with the Pedagogical Lead.

A lack of access to continuing professional development to support gaps in knowledge in skill, will leave educators demotivated and lacking in confidence.

Systems and resources

Regardless of whether the early childhood service adopts a digital documentation system or has a paper-based system, the key is **consistency and application**.

The early childhood service should adopt a documentation system that is individual to the child, embedded in practice, and where all elements of documentation link together and complement each other.

This includes observation, learning stories and curriculum planning which are **connected and progressive**.

The system and the documentation expectations of early childhood should be communicated to educators and appropriate time to document and reflect should be part of the daily routine. The lack of time and a consistent recording tool can lead to weakened teamwork, inconsistency in practice and differing outcomes for individual children.

Documentation is a powerful pedagogical tool to support children's learning. Nevertheless, its application should not be taken lightly.

Effective application requires diligence on behalf of the educator – to understand it, to self-reflect and to grow in skill.

It also requires professional pedagogical tools and a support framework to be put in place by the early childhood setting for educators to develop and learn this important skill.

CHAPTER 3

Documentation isn't an optional extra

A STORY OF LEARNING

I have experienced pedagogical documentation to be one of the most insightful and effective teaching and learning strategies that educators have at their disposal. It gives the educator a mechanism to view babies, toddlers and young children through a meaningful lens and transform how they 'see' and support learning and development. Educators capture information in different ways and use it to inform pedagogical practice such as observation, assessment, reflection, curriculum planning and reflection.

To undervalue documentation practice, to view it as an administration chore, or as an accountability mechanism for outside bodies; does a great disservice to this powerful pedagogical strategy. Not to mention the young child.

This chapter highlights why documentation should not be considered as an 'optional extra' in early childhood practice, and instead represents the very essence of slow pedagogy and meaningful, child-inspired practice.

Child documentation in early education

Whilst the focus here is on **pedagogical documentation**, it is important to highlight that documentation has different functions for early education. These can be categorised under 3 broad headings - *Documentation of Care, Documentation of Learning* and *Documentation to share Information*.

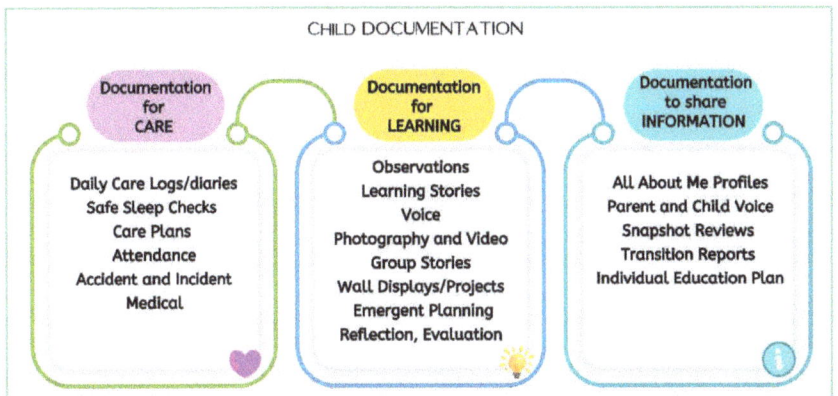

Documentation of Care includes record keeping around the personal care and needs of babies, toddlers and young children. This may include recording daily care routines, safe sleep checks, attendance or medical information. Educators' complete documentation of care records on a daily basis or as required. It is important that educators implement protocols for care recording as these records are often part of **regulatory compliance and child safety** in early childhood settings. In the event of an investigation, care records can provide vital evidence of good practice.

Documentation for Learning, or pedagogical documentation, concerns how educators use multiple ways of capturing learning episodes or interactions while children play, making early learning visible. The process and effectiveness of pedagogical documentation is considered an early education **quality indicator**.

Documentation for sharing information concerns any information that is useful when a child is transitioning from one place to another, or when specific information about a child's learning and development is required to provide external professional support (for example, an Individual Education Plan). This includes the child's perspective as appropriate.

The functions of documentation for learning

Broadly speaking, there are two types of assessment used in early education - assessment of learning and assessment for learning.

Firstly, Assessment for Learning describes assessment that happens **during the process of learning**, on a number of occasions rather than at the end. Assessment for Learning is not about making comparative judgements. It is about recognising, analysing and supporting learning over time. This is known as **formative assessment**.

Secondly, *Assessment of Learning* is usually summative, meaning that an assessment is carried out at the end of a period of time. Summative assessment involves stepping back to gain an overview of children's development and progress - for example, in a **transition report** or **snapshot review** covering a particular time period.

It is worth pointing out that **reliable summative assessment** (for example, information on transition reports) is not an assessment in itself. Rather, the summative information stems from **progressive methods of ongoing formative assessment**.

What is pedagogical documentation?

'Pedagogical Documentation' sounds formal, but it is quite simple.

It describes how, as part of everyday practice, educators use observation and engagement techniques to make sense of children's interests and interactions during play.

The starting point for meaningful, child inspired documentation is the educator's view of the child. This includes recognition that the child is actively involved in shaping their own learning, they are individuals with a life story, they can communicate in many ways, and have a right to have their voice heard and responded to.

The roots of pedagogical documentation

Pedagogical documentation has its roots in the world famous municipal of early childhood services in Reggio Emilia, Northern Italy (Giudici, C., C. Rinaldi and M. Krechevsky, eds. (2001) and in the Learning Story approach used in New Zealand (Ministry of Education, 2017).

Pedagogical documentation is defined as *'material communication tools appropriated or developed by teachers/practitioners or researchers for the purpose of recalling, reflecting on, re-thinking and re-shaping learning, teaching, knowledge and understanding'* (Carr et al., 2016: 277).

Effective documentation practice takes place over time and in a variety of social and environmental contexts, for example, indoors and outdoors, alone and with others, during different play contexts and discussions, and when engaging with different activities.

Dalberg and Moss view pedagogical documentation as an *'extraordinary tool for dialogue, for exchange, for sharing'* which requires *'a collective and democratic process of interpretation, critique and evaluation, involving dialogue and argumentation, listening and reflection, from which understandings are deepened and judgements are co-constructed'* (2007, p23).

Information gathered authentically as children engage with stimulating invitations to play, demonstrates the richness of what they know and can do, their strengths, opinions, choices and interests. This ongoing collection of information gradually builds a holistic pattern of babies, toddlers and young children as participative learners with unique **learning dispositions, skills, attitudes, knowledge and understanding.**

Multi-modal documentation

The Learning Story Approach (Carr 2001) and the Mosaic Approach (Clark 2017) have been hugely influential in shaping multi-modal methods of documenting the learning of babies, toddlers and young children.

The Mosaic Approach (Clark, 2017) offers a framework for listening to children's perspectives. Clark (2017) describes the Mosaic Approach as a 'multi-method, polyvocal approach that brings together different perspectives to create *with* children, an image of their worlds' (p17). Used mainly as a framework for listening to children during the research process, elements of the approach have much to lend to **participatory documentation practice.**

Multi-modal documentation is used to describe how educators make learning visible through a variety of **modes** that include narrative, audio, video, imagery and include multiple perspectives including children, family, educators and other professionals.

Digital documentation

Documentation practices are undergoing a significant change as paper-based practice becomes increasingly digitised.

The advent and availability of digital media has considerably expanded the multi-modality of documentation options including interactive and online functions.

More and more educators are understanding the **single dimension limitations** of paper portfolios and scrapbooks. By contrast, digital documentation creates **multi-modal representations** of child-led learning through learning stories, video and audio recordings, photovoice, child voice and family voice.

Formosinho and Pascal (2017) support the multiple-voice perspective of digital documentation commenting that *'there is value in documentation which captures and interweaves the voices of educators, parents and children, where 'voice' should be considered broadly, beyond speech, to acknowledge the multimodal nature of communication'*.

Digital documentation is a pedagogical tool, enabling 'in the moment' recordings of key learning moments including learning that may otherwise be missed.

Other advantages include digital documentation creating a record that is widely shareable and expediting the documentation process for educators saving valuable time and resources.

Also, some families may be more inclined to engage with documentation if it is accessible in real time on their smartphone or tablet. Cowan & Flewitt, (2021) highlight the child and family agency potential of digital documentation and comment that *'digital documentation opens possibilities for capturing the dynamic and embodied vibrancy of young children's learning and can make children's documentation more accessible to children and their parents'.*

A small cluster of children actively engaging with the class digital storybooks on MOSAIC Educator.

This experience supports the **technological empowerment** *of young children by using technology in a meaningful way.*

Accessibility is achieved by educators using a digital device to engage children with their unique e-storybook/portfolio in areas such as **self-reflection, self-assessment and small group discussion**.

This practice not only grows children's awareness of the meaningful use of technology, but it also builds self-esteem through **celebrating and reflecting on achievements**. This is further reinforced at home when parents receive learning stories, pictures and videos through an interlinked application in real time.

The use of video, particularly for educators to rewatch short video clips of natural play interactions or episodes, enables the educator to 'slow down' the observation and consider the child's play in greater detail. Small details can be missed in a busy room.

Therefore, video will enable the educator to focus on the detail which may have been missed in a real-time observation. This is significant for children who may be more difficult to observe to produce meaningful learning observations.

Cowan and Flewitt (2021:p15) support this assertion. They call for raised awareness of children whose multi-modal signs of learning may be harder to observe and document in traditional paper-based documentation, and calls for forms of observation and documentation that *'draw attention to the subtleties of children's silent and embodied signs of learning, as well as their more tangible displays'*.

*Using the MOSAIC class storybook, the educator **'slows down' reflects and discusses** play episodes using videos and photographs to bring children's learning to life.*

A Socio-cultural approach to assessment

Pedagogical documentation represents an inclusive definition. And one which imbues **environmental and situational context, process and participation**.

Whilst documentation focuses on the individual child, in line with a socio-cultural perspective for learning, it is important to draw on observations of children in various **social and environmental contexts**. For example, in learning situations where children interact with peers, with adults or as part of a group. Also, considering actions indoors and outdoors and with various play resources, tools and devices.

This **participatory method of documentation** moves away from the traditional educational focus of 'before and after' summative assessment where generic indicators are used to 'measure children's achievements' – frequently due to a focus on accountability or school readiness. Ongoing documentation allows for more **democratic evaluative processes** to understand and validate young children's learning experiences and interactions within the environment in which they play and learn.

The starting point

A common misconception regarding documentation is that it is something carried out **after** learning has taken place. This is not the case. The positioning of documentation **within**, and **as part of**, pedagogical practice is crucially important.

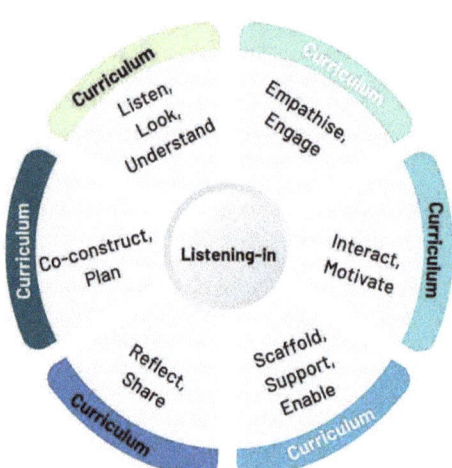

The **starting point** for meaningful documentation for learning is to listen-in to the child and use a variety of supportive responses and engagement strategies. This will garner information to inform curriculum planning and progress learning.

For example, observing a toddler working through a rotation schema, will lead the educator to scaffold, support and enable further opportunities to explore rotation processes *(see 'Exploring how circles work' learning story on the next page)*. This then feeds into the emergent curriculum plan making planning **meaningful and child-inspired**.

Guided by the goals of the early childhood curriculum, this informed approach to participative documentation leads to the provision of **time sensitive** learning opportunities for children.

*CJ's story **'Exploring how circles work'** created on MOSAIC Educator, **demonstrates an interest in circles and rotation**. In this tri-part learning story the educator succinctly describes what was observed, then summarises learning and uses the child's perspective to inform adults about the further activities that will support progression in learning around CJ's special interest.*

 CJ
Posted on 11... Read by parent

CJ spent a long time today drawing circles, adding face features and making marks. He was absorbed for at least 15 minutes, working quietly and with purpose. He frequently changed marker colours and diligently replaced the tops as he worked. He navigated drawing space on the page, filling in empty spaces and creating repeat images using both fine and large motor movements.

Exploring how circles work

Where did it take place: Creative table

Learning goals achieved:

1. I am making decisions and choices about my own learning and development.
2. I am discovering, exploring and refining my gross and fine motor skills.
3. I enjoy being creative.
4. I use mark-making to show meaning.
5. I can concentrate and I am purposeful and absorbed in my play.
6. I am demonstrating positivity in my own abilities.

Dispositions

 Exploring Symbols
Pattern Creativity

You can help me build on this by:

I am interested in rotation and how this works. I am showing you this interest through my drawings. Build on my understanding by giving me things with wheels and cogs to play with, let me draw circles in sand and with paint, let me roll hoops and give me objects that spin, give me old bracelets, bangles and cd's to explore, give me windmills and spinners to observe in the wind, and help me make a ribbon stick to rotate... these things will help me learn more about my special interest in circles and things that rotate.

Educator: RS... Toddler Room

What makes documentation meaningful?

Effective documentation practice requires an understanding of the importance of **reality, meaning and context** to the lived experiences of the child. Like adults, children are at their best when they are interested and motivated. Children engage and learn when things are meaningful and real to them.

Play experiences should be differentiated, reflect the child's **age, ability and lived experience**. Within this context, documentation meets the child where they are at and is **progressive over time** - slowly and progressively building skills, knowledge and positive dispositions.

Documentation tells the story of how learning came about. This helps capture the **process of learning, the place and time and who was involved**. The ongoing observation and documentation of children's reactions whilst engaged in meaningful play activities and situations is the most reliable way of building a picture of what children can do. It does not pass unsubstantiated judgement but instead focuses on where learning can go with educator and family support.

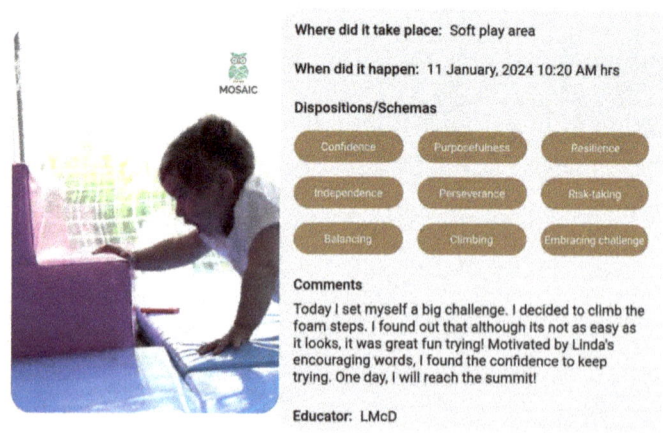

THIS IS MY LIVED EXPERIENCE..

I am 10 months old. I can **communicate** through my **behaviour, vocalisations, gestures and actions**.

I am telling you that I am cared for. I know what it's like to be gently held and fed as I can **model** this behaviour with my doll.

I am valued because I know to look at my doll and **pay attention** when I am feeding her.

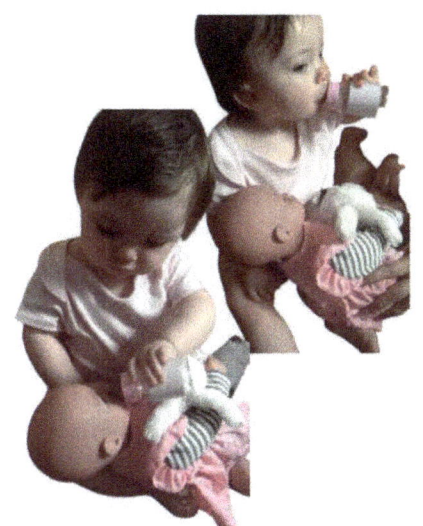

This is my **lived experience** so I can **recall the experience, replicate the experience and understand the experience**.

Support me by **validating** my play, **acknowledge** that I am gentle and caring with my doll, **ask** me questions and **model** new words and phrases. **Sing** a short song or rhyme that I can sing to my doll. **Display** these photos where I can see them so that I can look at them later and **recall my play**.

Reality and perspectives

Sometimes we need a little reminder that our reality is not always children's reality or perspective. Engaging with children never fails to reveal this. On the next page are two short stories that reminded me of this recently. Both stories came from spending time with my 5-year-old grandson.

IT'S REAL TO ME..

How do you spell your name?

A-V-R-I-L

(Writes the letters and looks at them intently)
It doesn't look right- what does that say?

It says Avril

No, how do you spell your real name - Nana?

N-A-N-A

IMPORTANT WORDS..

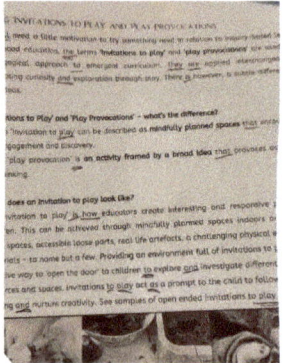

For a time, he watches me intently as I proofread a chapter for this book. I purposely ignore and let him observe. Eventually he asks, **'Why are you drawing lines under words?'**

I tell him because some of the words are especially important so I'm putting a line under them to remind me.

I give him a draft chapter and a pen. He purposefully scans the page and starts to underline words.

After a while, I asked him why he was selecting certain words. **'These are my key reading words in school- they are important words too'**.

And they are - to him.

Meaningful image displays, placed at a level where children can see and interact with them, provide children with a **visual sense of identity**, *place and belonging that extends beyond the family tree –*

'We are from this place'.

Images courtesy of Little Stars Pre-school, Moville, Co. Donegal

Multiple benefactors

Whilst there are different benefactors from the documentation process, it is essential that documentation is principally for the benefit of the **child**.

Let's consider the different ways that documentation can benefit different partners in the early education process.

Documentation supports the child
Children benefit from documentation because it:
- Enables child participation through voice, reflection and discussion regardless of age or ability.
- Shows the process of learning, preferred learning style, interests and individuality.
- Provides a connection between home and school.
- Focuses on the positives, building self-confidence and esteem.

Documentation gives learning structure
Learning aims and goals of the early childhood curriculum serve as guidelines for what is appropriate in terms of learning and development. Documentation for Learning:
- Aligns episodes of learning to curriculum goals, dispositions and skills.
- Provides a way to evaluate progress in learning and development.
- Shows strengths and areas to focus on within the curriculum planning cycle.

Documentation supports the educator

- Enables the educator to listen-in to the child – their strengths, needs and preferences.
- Enhances and focuses communication with parents.
- Guides curriculum planning and reflection processes.
- Makes learning visible for external compliance bodies.
- Allows educators to self-reflect on their pedagogical practice.

Documentation engages parents and family

- Builds a respectful partnership with educators and with the school, and
- Involves family in the child's learning and development.
- Shares critical learning periods to enable parents to reinforce at home.
- Demonstrates their child's capabilities.
- Provides talking points for parent-child conversations and self-esteem building at home.

Some documentation errors

The wise adage, 'Quality over Quantity' particularly applies to pedagogical documentation. The key here is to ensure that learning updates are **meaningful and relevant to the child**. Some common errors to avoid include:

- Creating updates and entries for the sake of it. The idea is to capture meaningful learning episodes, not the daily routine.

- Time gaps in updates and progression in learning are not visible.

- Only using photographs that are picture perfect – use images that show natural and spontaneous play and learning.

- Not using documented stories to reflect on prior experiences and celebrate achievements with children.

- Trying to apply multiple learning goals to the tri-part learning story – less is more.

- Not asking children for their permission or consent to take photographs or videos – educators need to act as role models for respectful use of digital devices.

- Documentation only features the educator's voice.

- Learning updates to parents are not shared in real-time.

- Documentation is not consistent or systematic and takes up a disproportionate amount of time.

- Educator supports, training and tools are not available.

*Multi-modal documentation acts like a vibrant kaleidoscope to **see, interpret and respond** to children's interests, preferences, abilities and needs.*

*It is essential that educators appreciate the **interdependency** of documentation to **child-inspired curriculum planning** and implementation.*

*There is no room for ambiguity. **Documentation isn't an optional extra.***

CHAPTER 4
What's the story?

A STORY OF LEARNING

Over 20 years ago, I first discovered the work of Dr. Margaret Carr on the Learning Story Approach. I soon realised her work held the key to authentic child-centred assessment for learning that easily married with a child-inspired curriculum for all children. Promoting the use of Learning Stories as a democratic and participative method of assessment in early education has been part of my work since that time.

This chapter considers the characteristics and strengths of the learning story approach when used as part of the documentation process of babies, toddlers and young children's learning.

The Learning Story Approach

Learning Stories emerged from the work of Dr Margaret Carr in New Zealand and are the adopted assessment response to the Te Whāriki early childhood curriculum.

Carr's Learning Story Approach foregrounds the child's dispositions to learn and reflects a socio-cultural view in which assessment is both situated and distributed across people, places and things (Cowie and Carr, 2004). Overall, this method relies on multiple perspectives and contexts including the child, the educator, family and environment.

Learning Stories capture the uniqueness of the individual child. Further, a picture is revealed of a positive image of babies, toddlers and young children as **participative learners** with distinctive strengths, abilities and interests.

The approach considers learning as a process or a journey, which changes over time. Reflections are therefore made over a prolonged period **as part of** the pedagogical documentation process.

Creating learning stories

The educator observes children's play, takes notes, photographs or video of a play scenario. Then constructs short stories about what they noticed.

Typically, stories reflect **the learning episode, learning achieved and a plan for progression**. Learning Stories promote an equitable approach to formative assessment. Regardless of a child's age, ability or mode of communication, learning stories **start with where the child is at**, and what makes them unique. Stories communicate much more than a level of achievement. They communicate the distinctive position of the child including their **interests, preferences, abilities and needs**.

A Learning Story can be created from two scenarios. Either a planned observation (where the early childhood educator plans to assess the child's progress in relation to a specific skill or learning goal), or a spontaneous snapshot of a learning episode or conversation.

Learning stories should be clear, to the point, informative and need not be long.

Learning stories should not be overpopulated with multiple learning goals as this dilutes the succinct messaging of the learning story itself. Learning goals highlighted should be **visible** in the learning episode, video or photographs.

As Learning stories include a plan to support and consolidate learning, this is what makes them an important assessment for learning mechanisms for educators. When narrative learning stories are used as a component of multi-modal forms of documentation like imagery, videos, or creative examples, **a revealing image of the child** as a participative and unique learner is formed.

A SUITCASE FULL OF STORIES

In Asha's story **'Tickly Teeth'**, note that the educator has only highlighted the learning goals that relate directly to the discussion. Also note the multiple voices in the story - educator, child and family.

Tickly teeth!

Asha, you told me all about your visit to the dentist yesterday.
'The dentist was a girl and she had a tiny mirror on a stick to see my teeth at the back. She looks after everybodys teeth and fixes them if they go black '.

Wow, what else happened?

'She squirted air into my teeth and it tickled.. It was funny! I am going to brush my teeth every morning and every night to keep them white - not black'.

What a great plan Asha!

Learning goals achieved:

1 I am demonstrating positive attitudes to hygiene and routine.
2 I am confident.
3 I am learning to build respectful relationships with others.
4 I am developing my understanding about the different roles of people in my community.
5 I can use an expanding vocabulary of words and phrases, and show a growing understanding of sentence structure.

Dispositions/Schemas

Sociability    Communication   Language

You can help me build on this by:

One of my key strengths and favourite way of learning is through language and discussion.
Let me tell you more stories about my experiences and support me to draw pictures and find books on the areas I talk about.Teach me tongue twisters, rhymes and songs.

Encourage me to listen and take turns in conversation - especially during small group activities.

Educator: CR

Parent's comment

She was very brave for her first visit- great that she is telling you all about it! .. Meave x

Capturing multiple voices

Learning stories can include multiple voices involved in the learning episode. This could be the child's actual explanation of a piece of artwork or construction, the educator's interpretation, or a summary of a conversation between the educator and child or between two children.

The educator can convey child voice in a variety of ways through learning story documentation (see Chapter 5: The Voice Box). For example, when the child finds something of interest or achieves something they set out to do, the educator can convey their expressions, comments or behaviour.

Child voice can also be included in the curriculum planning process. (See Chapter 9).

Taking time to engage and reflect on learning stories with children, can provide meaningful insights for the educator and spark ideas for further child-led activities.

Parent/Family voice in the form of a comment added in response to a learning story, adds another voice to the documented learning episode. Also, a relevant comment or information shared by a parent or family member can be **crafted into a learning story** to provide meaningful connections for the child.

Another means of including multiple voices is if an outside professional is involved with the child's care, learning and development in any way. In this situation, any commentary made by an outside professional can be used to add another perspective. For example, as part of a transition report or review.

THE LEARNING STORY CYCLE

The learning story cycle

The potential of a learning story as a pedagogical strategy is revealed by following a simple 4 stage process - **Create, Communicate, Consolidate and Connect**. When used by the educator, this cycle has the power to capture, validate, progress, and share learning.

- Firstly, the educator **creates** the learning story based on an observation and analysis of the child's play and learning.

- The educator then **communicates** the story by reading it either to the child or to a small group of children in an age-appropriate way. The educator draws attention to the child's actions and words as well as pictures or video captured as part of the story. Sharing stories can spark ideas from other children and encourage children to think and reflect.

- **Consolidate** learning and support progress by noting extension ideas for the emergent plan. Discuss with children and other colleagues what additional materials could be used or what the group could find out more about.

- **Connect** with family by sharing the story in real time. Stories are meaningful to family and connect in a way that is more meaningful than a score or a checklist of skills. Invite family to share their comments about the story to encourage engagement.

What makes learning stories different?

The speciality of Learning Stories is that they provide an **equitable documentation system** for all children. The strengths-based perspective used in learning stories can transform how children who are neurodiverse are viewed as learners. Stories highlight **unique interests, learning styles and preferences** and these are used positively to show how learning takes place.

The potential of learning stories to enable children to participate in the documentation process is endless. The inclusion of the child's translated or actual voice in learning stories together with the ability to use learning stories as a mechanism to revisit and reflect on learning contributes greatly to participative documentation.

Many vibrant details can be included in the learning experience of the child including the magical and vibrant learning process and the people and situations involved in this process. Stories can include interactions, multiple voices, interests, dispositions, and humour. Together with the ability to link to and inform emergent curriculum planning, this makes learning stories an ideal way of documenting children's views, choices and experiences as a unique and participative learner. The strengths of the approach are outlined in the diagram *'Learning Story Key Strengths'*.

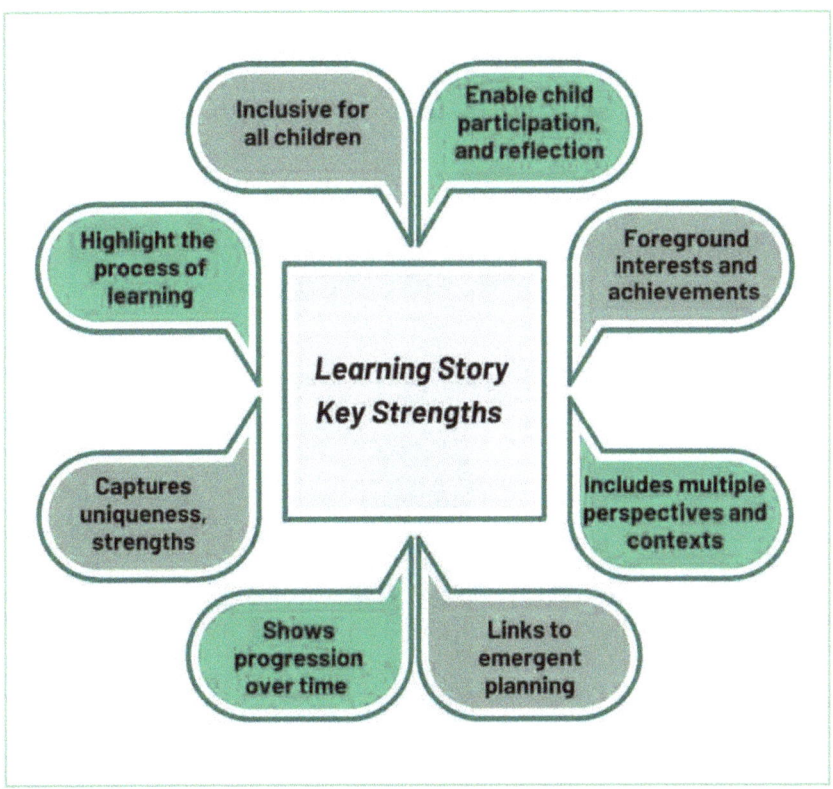

What can different learning stories look like?

Learning Stories can be presented in a variety of formats and used in conjunction with multiple modes of documentation.

By using a combination of different modes over time, a portrait of early learning evolves – telling the story of when learning happened, who was involved, what learning was achieved and how learning was supported. This ensures that pedagogical documentation is socio-cultural in approach and implementation.

The secret is to use a combination of different story types. When educators draw on a variety of learning story formats, the combined collective of narrative, video, imagery and voice, spans multiple dimensions; simultaneously building an insightful picture of the child's reality, position and progress.

Even very young children are **digitally aware**. A favourite activity at this early childhood setting is when children get the opportunity to share their learning stories with family through the MOSAIC application.

1. Tri-part stories

The Tri-part Learning Story is structured in 3 interlinking components. This includes **a learning episode** which is a succinct narrative of a learning engagement observed, **a summary of learning** observed in the story and **a plan for progression.** Educators use photographs, copies of children's work and comments from parents to support the written narrative. The Tri-part story contains the information needed to transform the observation into documentation for learning.

2. Stories that document the visual process of learning

Photographs and videos can be used as a quick and efficient way of keeping a child's learning portfolio current, visual, and engaging. Where possible, children should be enabled to document examples of their creative work or constructions themselves by using digital cameras. A brief comment from the educator or a transcribe of the child's description of their work can be added to provide context to the learning episode.

> *Multi-modal recordings offer a holistic perspective of the individual child and in turn provides the educator with constructive insight. This makes learning stories a pivotal and far-reaching scaffold from which to support and propel learning and development.*

Group/Living Wall projects that take place over time can be documented in hallways or at low level in the room. These projects usually build over time, adding new photographs, items of interest, creative work and commentary from different children as the project evolves.

3. Stories that summarise learning after a specific period of time

Stories that summarise learning at different intervals fall under the category of 'Assessment of Learning'. This means that the process of learning is not explained, it is a summary of what the child has achieved as framed by learning goals of the early childhood curriculum. These include Snapshot Reviews or Individual Education Plans to reflect on progress over a specific period or Transition Reports for when a child moves from one location to another. These summary stories should include some form of target setting for the next timeframe or stage in the child's learning journey. Summary reports should include multiple perspectives, including the child's voice where possible.

Are anecdotal observations and pictures enough?

To observe children is a crucial component of early childhood practice. This can be carried out on an anecdotal basis during play. However, an observation in isolation is of limited use. It is only when an observation is surrounded by additional modes of documentation or developed into Tri-part learning stories that it becomes a pedagogical tool to recognise, respond to and support learning.

A sporadic collection of photographs in a scrapbook with examples of art and craft is useful as a memento for parents at the end of the year, or a floor-book for children to use for reflection and discussion. However, this should not be confused with systematic documentation to support children's progress in learning through a linked cycle of listening, planning, documenting and reflecting *(See Chapter 9 for more)*.

A SUITCASE FULL OF STORIES

Macey's story 'It all looks nice now' is a good example of how the educator **notices** Macey's interest in the shop, then observes her interest in **sorting and classifying**. By doing this, the educator recognises a good 'hook' for a learning story that is connected to learning goals and dispositions. The educator plans activities using Macey's interest and will reflect on her progression by continuing this cycle.

'It all looks nice now..'

Macey is spending lots of time in the shop. She selects items and sorts them into different baskets. "I am putting all the potatoes together.. then I'm going to put all the bananas and apples together".

Macey arranged various items by type and colour, focusing on the task in hand and advising her friends 'I am tidying the shop to make it nice, it looks nice now" Macey stands back and smiles at her work. What great organisational skills you have Macey!

Dispositions/Schemas

- Purposefulness
- Voice
- Classifying
- Ordering
- Pattern

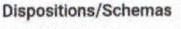

MOSAIC

You can help me build on this by:
I am interested in ordering and classifying objects. Give me a variety of loose parts to explore and continue my interest in this mathematical concept. Talk to me about patterns, groups, characteristics of objects, similarity and difference.

What to look for when creating a learning story - finding the 'HOOK'

To create learning stories that are focussed and progressive, a useful technique is when the educator can recognise a good 'Hook' for the story. The 'Hook' is something that educators learn to recognise before committing an observation to a learning story. The hook connects with key learning goals and dispositions and gives the educator something to build the story on and take forward.

Some of the behaviours that the educator can look out that signify a hook include:

- **Self-initiated:** Play comes from the child's own interests, ideas or explorations. For example, the child is building something unique from loose parts.

- **Engagement:** The child is engaged and the play episode is sustained for a period of time. For example, the toddler is repeatedly lining different objects up, focusing for a sustained period.

- **Purposeful:** The child demonstrates intention, perseverance, or has a plan in mind. The baby is determined to get to the top of the foam step, despite many repeated tries.

- **Relationships:** The child is interacting and engaging with others. For example, forming close friendships and playing cooperatively.

- **Responsive:** The toddler responds to a provocation displayed/placed in the room.

- **Progressive:** The baby demonstrates a new achievement or a skill is attained at a higher level.

- **Recalling or Connecting:** Making a connection or recalling a previous learning experience.

- **Learning:** Positive dispositions, skills, attitudes, knowledge and understanding. For example, the baby, toddler or young child shows progression in learning in any area of well being, learning or development.

> *Stories help us to **look closely at learning** and see the process unfold.*
>
> *Stories depicted through imagery, narrative, and child voice, have the power to evoke emotion, afford context, and deliver meaning.*
>
> *Learning stories are **emotionally persuasive**, therefore they engage everyone involved - the child, educators, and family, on a deeper level.*

CHAPTER 5
The Voice Box

A STORY OF LEARNING

Over the years, I have witnessed many different interpretations of child voice, and have always found educators willing to embrace this practice in the documentation process. Educators who incorporate child voice in its most effective form, are those who appreciate the enabling factors that have to be in place to ensure that child voice is heard and responded to.

In addition, those educators who appreciate the subtle differences in writing techniques, and how this influences perspective, can increase the visibility of children in the documentation process.

Grounded by the child's right to participate, this chapter introduces the 'Voice Box' - five different writing techniques to increase the visibility of the child in story narratives. Each narrative style within the Voice Box is brought to life through practical examples of its application to learning stories.

Participation, voice and perspective

Including the voice of the child is not a new consideration for early education.

This originates from Article 12 of The United Nations (UN) Convention on the Rights of the Child (1989) which states that children have the right to have their opinions considered and their views respected in decision-making that affects them (UN, 1989).

In early education, this can be accomplished in a variety of ways using child-led techniques and practice. This includes by educators actively listening-in to babies, toddlers and young children, **valuing their choices and preferences**, providing **equitable learning environments** and by **responding to their needs and rights** within the realms of their well being and safety.

This speaks to the Lundy (2007) child-rights model of participation which identifies four key components that need to be in place to **enable** child participation:

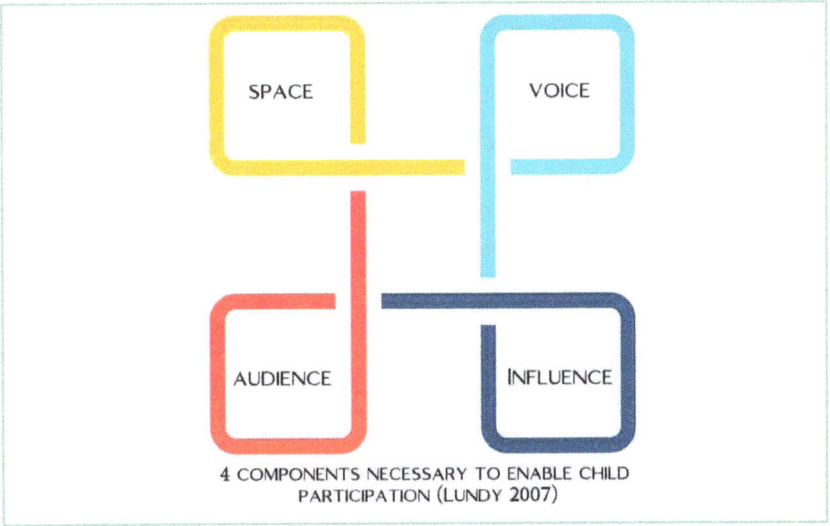

4 COMPONENTS NECESSARY TO ENABLE CHILD PARTICIPATION (LUNDY 2007)

- **Space:** Children must be given the opportunity to express a view (documentation practice for the individual child).

- **Voice:** Children must be facilitated to express their views (modes of child voice included).

- **Audience:** The view must be listened to (adults listen).

- **Influence:** The view must be acted upon, as appropriate (meaningful response).

Child perspective and child voice through documentation

The documentation process itself plays an **enabling role** in including child voice in early learning experiences for babies, toddlers and young children.

When used appropriately, a huge advantage of using multi-modal documentation is that it actively involves the child in the documentation process. In addition, it enables them to be an **active participant** in their own decision making, learning and reflection.

A documentation system focusing on the **individual child**, provides the **Space** to consider child voice.

The inclusion of oral or other modes of voice in the documentation and reflection provides a mechanism to **see and hear Voice**. The component of **Audience** is enabled through sharing stories, work and updates with other educators, family and other professionals.

And finally, **Influence** is included in the documentation process by ensuring that the observed needs and rights of the child are **responded to** by informing emergent curriculum planning and decision making.

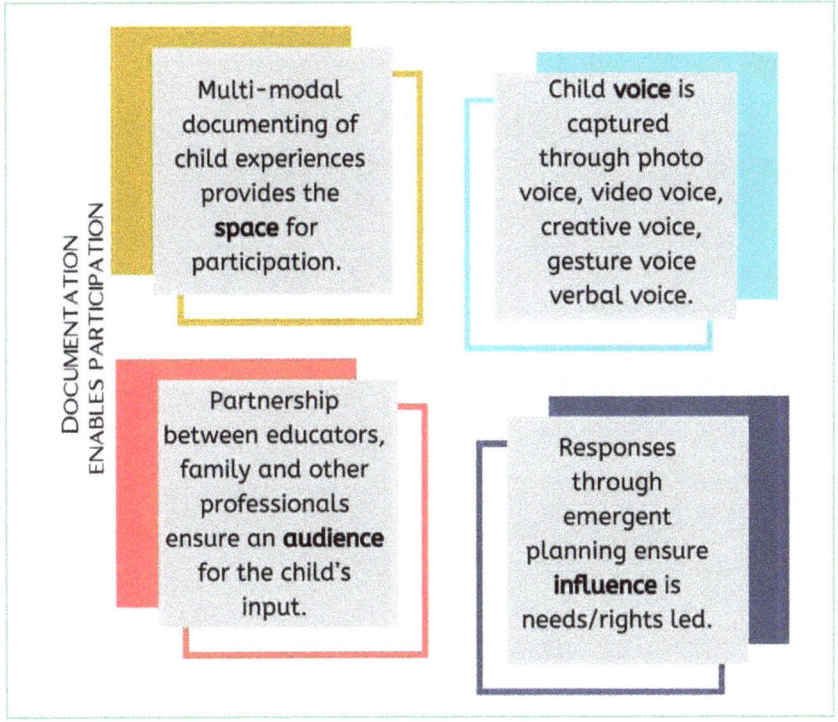

The time and skill of the proficient educator is paramount in being able to see and hear the child's preferences and voice regardless of their mode of communication.

The most important verbs in early education are not 'to talk', 'to teach' or 'to show' – but to **'listen-in'**.

This practice is not confined to children who have spoken language.

Children of all ages and abilities show us many signs. We need to know what to look for to translate the **multi-modal language of the child**. And translate this in a way that is **visible and engaging**.

The *'My View'* story *'Snuggle Naps'* captured on MOSAIC, allows the educator to document and share Freddie's sleep preferences.

This demonstrates how baby Freddie's voice seen through his behaviours, gestures and preferred routines are recognised, respected and acted upon.

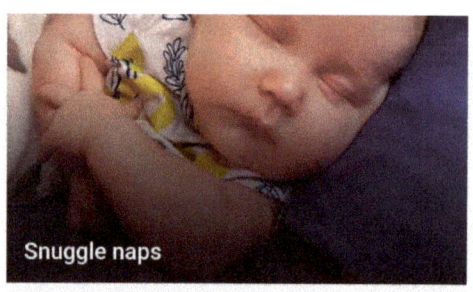

Snuggle naps

Date and time: 22 June, 2022 10:05 AM hrs

MOSAIC

I took these pictures because...

This picture shows my preferred sleep comfort object - my cuddle blanket.

This makes me feel...

I would like to...

I smell and stroke the blanket as I drift off to sleep. I show that I am content as I hum to myself.

You can help me build on this by...

Give me the words associated with sleep, sing to me as I drift off. Ensure that my cuddle blanket is available for naps.

Comments

Freddie is asserting his preferred routine for sleep. He knows what soothes him and what helps him feel secure and relaxed.

This quick **Picture Story *'Looking for fish'*** reaches out to Asha's family about her nature walk by the river. The story, sent electronically to family in real time, creates an important **discussion point** between Asha and her family when she returns home. This builds Asha's sense of **connection between home and the early childhood service**. Via this story, Asha is receiving positive messages that **her experiences and reflections about her day are important** to all the adults in her life.

This nurtures her sense of **belonging and strengthens her self-image**.

*This story is brief, but it tells us a lot. We know that Asha was given the **'space'** to ask questions and was able to **'voice'** a suggestion for her next trip to the river. She was able to relay her experience to her family. This has given her a wider **'audience'** for her ideas, and will **'influence'** the adults in her life to respond to her suggestions. This represents the enablers of child participation captured in a short picture story on MOSAIC Educator.*

Looking for fish

Where did it take place: Walk by the river

Where did it happen: 22 March, 2022 10:46 AM hrs

Dispositions

Interest   Imagination   Having fun
Voice   Exploring   Asking questions

Comments
Asha asked lots of questions today on our walk and was particularly interested in looking for fish in the river. She suggested we take a net on our next visit. Great idea Asha!

✓ Read by parent

Parent's comment: Oh she has talked about this non-stop since she came home! I have been told that we need to buy a fishing net but she only wants to look at the fish and will put them back into the river afterwards! Thank you for giving Asha this lovely experience.. Claire and Martin 😊

Educator's comment: Delighted that she enjoyed it so much and good luck with the fishing net shopping! 🐟

The Voice Box

The **'Voice Box'** classification is fundamental to the educators' understanding of the authenticity of child voice. Furthermore, it is essential to differentiate between **voice perspectives** and how they can be used to convey meaningful learning story narratives.

This section outlines five writing techniques that **emphasise the perspective of the child**, making babies, toddlers and young children **visible** in the documentation process.

The educator is the narrator of the child's story and uses writing techniques and imagery to interpret observations.

The story is written from a perspective of strength and highlights what the child is doing. There are different writing perspectives that you can use to convey child perspective in learning stories. This is largely down to personal choice and each method tells the story in a slightly different way as outlined in the examples that follow.

The five modes that educators can use include:

1. **Photo/Video voice** (see 'The REAL Camera').
2. **Translated Voice** - interpreting play (see 'Duck Duck').
3. **Partnership Voice** – co-constructing and listening (see 'Bubble Stuff').
4. **Verbal Voice** – the spoken word (see 'Different Colours').
5. **Interviewed Voice** - investigating perspectives (see 'Hungry Birds').

1. 'Photo Voice and Video Voice'
Powerful child-led actions to enable listening, understanding and change

Photo Voice has its roots in action research where marginalised individuals and groups are given the opportunity to take photographs. These photographs are used to promote dialogue to share and deepen understanding of an issue or concern and bring about change.

One cannot help drawing comparisons with the powerful potential of photography and videography as a **participatory method for young children in early childhood settings**. Photographs and videos have meaning for children's

lived experiences, and they already know that imagery has value in the adult world. They have seen family members take and view photographs and videos, and photographs are displayed in the home.

Photographs and video offer powerful **modes of language** for children as they can convey information through the **visual voice of the camera**. They employ imagery and discussion as a means for children to **express and deepen their understanding of an issue**, concern, or idea. The opportunity to explore with the digital camera, the images taken and the accompanying voice perspective from the child and the educator response, give 'Space, Voice, Audience and Influence' (Lundy 2007) to the learning experience.

Child 'Voice' in the context of photo/video voice can be used to give the child the right and opportunity to communicate a feeling or opinion in matters that impact on them. Photographs can be used for reflection with children and discuss ideas to bring about change. For example:
- What is important to the child.
- What the child's strengths are.
- What they like/dislike.
- What they are interested in.
- What they would like to change.
- Things they want to talk about.

> **'Photo Voice' and 'Video Voice'** *enable children to create symbolic representations to offer insight, communicate their experiences and help others see the world through their eyes. When used alongside narrative stories, this multi-modal, participative approach is unparalleled as authentic in child-led documentation.*

This *'My View'* story, captured on MOSAIC Educator, is a practical response to a child's right to participate.

In this story *'The REAL Camera',* the child's interest is sparked by using the real camera to take photographs of the leaves.

'My View' leaves no room for misinterpretation in terms of the inclusion of child voice employing **photo voice and communication.**

The unique and innovative perspective of the 'My View' story puts a spotlight on child-led participatory engagement.

2. 'Translated Voice'- interpreting interests

Translated Voice describes how unobtrusive or non-participatory observations carried out by the educator convey an interpretation of a child's work, play or communication.

This is used to communicate the child's interests or perspective on something. An example here would be an educator making an inference about the child's interest following an observation. Or an educator could add commentary to a photograph or piece of creative work.

For younger children or children using different modes of communication, Translated Voice can be used to document **gestures, sounds, facial expressions or play patterns** observed. Learning stories are an ideal way to capture Translated Voice.

To what extent the Translated Voice corresponds with the child's actual voice depends on several variables. This includes the extent to which the educator/researcher understands child development and multi-modal forms of communication. Also important is how well educators can empathise with and 'tune-in' to the child, their play patterns and behaviour.

Writing Perspectives for Translated Voice

Methods of using Translated Voice: Educators write learning story narratives 'to' the child, 'about' the child or 'from' the child as preferred. See the examples below:

- **Educator writes 'to' the child**
  Matthew, I watched you today as you designed and built a garage for your trucks with loose parts. You chose lots of interesting materials including cardboard tubes, wooden lollipop sticks and buttons to decorate your wonderful construction.

- **Educator writes 'about' the child**
  Matthew was very busy today working in the loose parts area. He selected lots of interesting materials including cardboard tubes, lollipop sticks and buttons to make a garage for his favourite trucks.

- **Educator writes 'from' the child's perspective**
  When playing with loose parts today I decided to build a garage for my trucks. I carefully looked at all the materials on offer and chose some cardboard tubes, lollipop sticks and buttons. I worked diligently sticking the tubes together and decorating my garage.

*The story of **'Duck Duck'** demonstrates how **Translated Voice** is used for a toddler story. The educator tells the story from the **child's perspective** to make the story engaging and meaningful to the reader.*

Note the ideas not only for the early childhood setting at the bottom of the story, but for parents and family too.

Duck Duck!

The story of Duck Duck..

What a challenging experience! The yellow duck in the water tray kept swimming away from me and I made all kinds of efforts to catch it! I reached, I splashed, I moved the water with my hands and I poured water from my watering can. I repeatedly said *'Duck Duck'* and gestured with my hands to let the duck know that I wanted to play! I figured out a very clever solution. I walked to the side of the tray and caught the duck off-guard - success at last!

I showed through my play that I can **direct my own explorations** and **persist with a challenge**. I used my **physical skills** and a range of **problem solving strategies** to reach the swimming duck! I used my **voice** and **waving gestures** in the hope that the duck would listen to me.

Play games with me and give me some fun challenges like beanbag throwing and hide and seek. **Praise my efforts** by clapping and overexaggerating facial expressions to show me that you approve of my efforts.

3. 'Partnership Voice' – co-constructing, communicating, listening

Partnership Voice describes observation, interaction and meaningful engagement where the child and the educator are involved in co-construction and collaboration of a learning experience.

Multi-modal communications between the educator and the child including facial expressions, gestures, verbal interactions or discussion between the educator and child which reveal the child's perspectives, understanding and choices.

An example could be photographs taken and described by children, collaborative drawing and creativity where the child has freedom to create from open ended materials or making a plan for the day.

Partnership Voice will ring bells with educators aware of **co-constructed learning and co-facilitation** in early education.

The **socio-cultural** idea of co-constructed learning is central to many aspects of early learning and is an insightful technique to use to relay a learning story. The **'turn-taking'** in conversation can relate to both verbal engagement (talking and listening, questions and answers) and non-verbal engagement (f or example, Peek a Boo or action songs and games).

Partnership Voice allows the educator to **probe**, to **make suggestions** and to **motivate** the child as the story unfolds. It also allows the educator to **validate** the child's own ideas and choices.

*Cassie's Picture Story **'Bubble Stuff'** is an example of **Partnership Voice** where the educator uses conversational turn taking to engage with Cassie and find out her thought processes.*

What's happening here Cassie?

I'm bursting the bubbles - the big ones

How did the bubbles get there?

They came from the bubble stuff..

Oh, I see - so what does the bubble stuff do?

It makes big bubbles and tiny ones in the water..

Do you think we could use the bubble stuff to wash our hands for snack now?

Yeah, then get snack.

Bubble Stuff!

4. Verbal Voice - talking

Verbal Voice is where the child's actual words as spoken are included in a learning story by the educator. Context can be provided by adding a sequence of photos. Alternatively, a voice recording or video can also capture the child's **actual words** as part of the learning story .

Using a child's 'Verbal Voice' is another way of bringing learning stories to life.

Using Verbal Voice to support photographic or videographic documentation in particular can be very powerful. The image will provide the visual representation of an idea, activity or behaviour and the child's words will bring this to authentic life.

*The story of **'Different Colours'** demonstrates how a combination of photo voice with verbal voice are used to document engagement with loose parts provocations*

Different colours..

'The paint is all different colours'
'I'm making a caravan'
'I am painting it all nice colours - like a rainbow'
'Yellow is my favourite'

5. Interviewed Voice- investigating perspectives

Interviewed Voice is where interaction and verbal communication is used to capture voice on a particular issue or matter.

Typically, a loosely structured discussion or interview in simple language is used to obtain the child's **thoughts and opinions**. This can be carried out in pairs or small groups. Again, the learning story format can be easily used to document Interviewed Voice.

'Interviewed Voice' is probably the most straightforward way of listening to children.

However, age and ability is a factor here as Interviewed Voice largely requires speech abilities. Again, the extent to which Interviewed Voice corresponds with actual voice greatly depends on interview style, the questions posed and how well children understand the questions or subject matter.

In addition, the extent to which voices are shaped to meet the adult objective is important when considering the authenticity of the child's Interviewed Voice.

'Hungry Birds and bright yellow stuff that tastes good'

Why should we feed the birds during winter do you think?

Jack 'because they have no food on the trees anymore'

Hannah 'they wait on their Mammy to feed them worms'

May 'They only have a tiny mouth'

Ok, can anyone think of some food that we could leave out to feed the birds so that they don't get hungry?

Michael 'Yeah, worms and cornflakes'

Jake 'Seeds'

Hannah – 'Balls that you buy in the shop'

Maura – 'Bright yellow stuff that tastes good'.

Fantastic thinking everyone! Ok, time to make a list of all the things we need to put our Hungry Birds plan into action!

*The learning story on the next page, created on **Mosaic Educator**, is used to **show progression** from the small group discussion (above) to the **implementation of the plan**. The educator uses the Group Learning Story to provide a snapshot of group learning and engagement with the activity and as **evidence** of emergent curriculum planning. This type of documentation also makes a useful addition to floor books so that children can **reflect on and discuss** past activities.*

Hungry Birds
Group Learning Story

We have gathered everything we need to make bird feeders - *'hmm..the peanut butter smells yummy'* says Harry!

Caring- Respect-Responsibility

We pat, roll, press and stick lots of seeds to pine cones and rolls. We discuss how the seeds feel between our fingers *'Bumpy'* says Orlagh. *'Spikey'* says Lilymay.

Socialability-Manipulating-Exploration

We tied our bird feeders to the trees. *'When will the birds come'* asks Jake.

We will just have to wait and see!

Excitement - Interest- Observation

Writing Perspectives are important

The 'Voice Box' classification provides a useful scaffold for educators and researchers from which to understand the quality and **authenticity of child voice**.

Photo Voice and Video Voice have wonderful creative potential and when adults give children the space to explore using photography and video making. This enables children to create symbolic representations to communicate their experiences and help others **see the world through their eyes**. This combined with the **expressive use of technology**, offers **limitless potential for experiential learning**.

The examples of **'Translated Voice'** highlight the **interpretation of the child's work or play**. The educator **'translates'** what is observed and crafts the learning story accordingly by using a preferred writing perspective. This can be either by speaking **'to'** the child, **'about'** the child or **'from'** the child's perspective.

The writing perspective of speaking 'to' the child and 'from' the child are **warmer in tone**.

This method makes stories more **emotionally engaging**. In addition, when you speak 'from' the child's perspective, you are highlighting the child's needs and rights to **all the adults in the child's life** (the audience).

The **'Partnership Voice'** promotes turn taking in conversation and both views are included. This demonstrates **co-facilitation and shared thinking** as a pedagogical strategy in early education.

'**Verbal Voice**' is where the educator records exactly what the child has said. This brings the child's **actual spoken voice and thought process** into stories which are authentic to the child.

'**Interview Voice**' is a question, probe and answer technique used with a small group of children when looking to increase participation, choice and decision making. This **engagement strategy** is useful in **small key person groups** to find out what children think or their opinions on something of interest.

> Although each voice type is distinct and different, a combination of voice types can be utilised in documentation practice. What is important is that educators understand how to make child voice *meaningful and visible* in the learning context.

CHAPTER 6
A collection of stories

A STORY OF LEARNING

I've witnessed documentation practice where educators capture learning stories in many different and creative ways. I find one of the things that make stories so unique is that some of them reveal not only the characteristics of the child, but of the educator too.

From a humorous episode that demonstrates personality and character strengths to an in-depth story of learning, all are equally valid. The pedagogical strength is in the way the story is used - to communicate with the child, consolidate learning and connect with family.

This chapter features a range of different learning stories about babies, toddlers and young children. A short explanation is provided under each story to bring to life some of the key features of meaningful pedagogical documentation.

A Storybook of Learning

There are many different learning story formats that educators can use to document children's interests, preferences, abilities and needs. It is useful to know what makes each story format different, and how to choose the format most suitable for the episode you want to document.

Some learning story formats are more suited to capturing a quick visual of an interaction or piece of work. Some require more detail to inform planning. And some others will provide an opportunity for the child to express their thoughts and opinions.

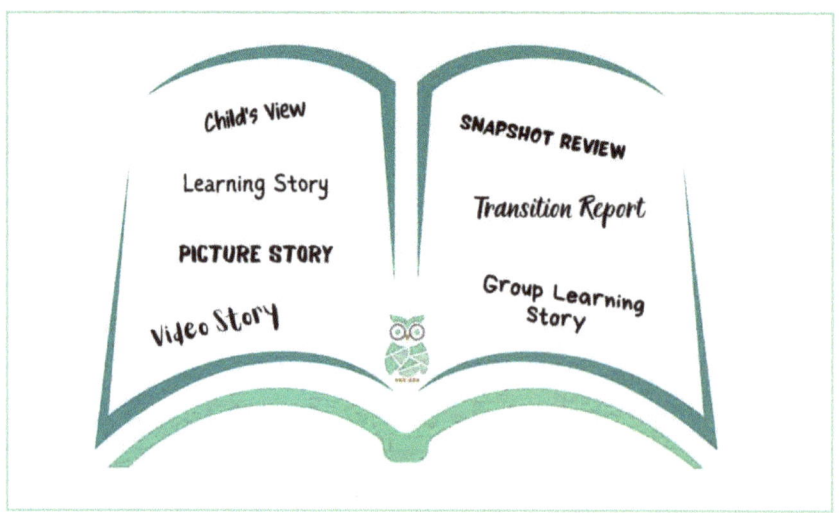

A collection of stories

Learning stories can be presented in different formats. The format itself is less important than the fundamentals that the story is strengths based, used to demonstrate the process of learning and support further learning. For example, MOSAIC Educator contains various story format options. In choosing a learning story format, educators have an idea about the purpose of the story, the time they have to document and the outcomes sought. *(Story formats highlighted below).*

Child's Voice Story (My View)
To include the child's actual voice, thoughts and choices regarding a particular area or idea.

Picture Story
To quickly capture and share a creation/interaction accompanied by a brief comment or observed disposition.

Snapshot Review:
A summary of progress and targets for a specific timeframe or an inhouse transition summary.

Group Story
To capture experiences for the whole group - use for a floor-book, display or planning evidence.

Transition Report
Summary of achievements so a new educator can provide consistency in learning and where the child can also have a say.

Tri-part Story
Record the early childhood curriculum learning goals achieved by the child and use this to inform a child-led curriculum plan.

Video Story
Capturing, slowing down and reflecting on children's play and learning.

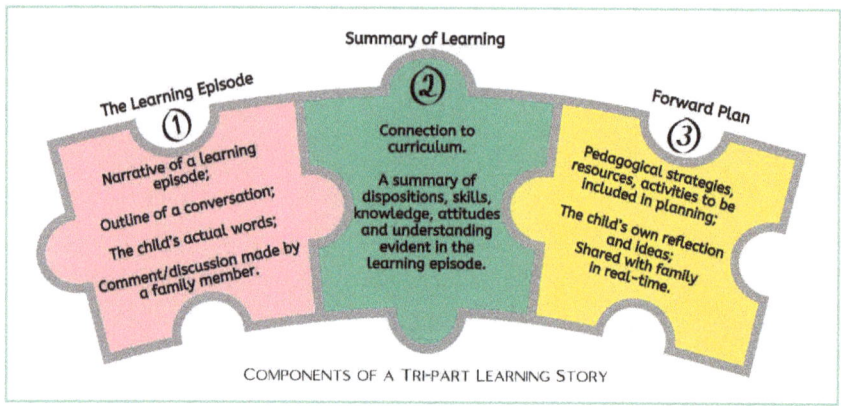

COMPONENTS OF A TRI-PART LEARNING STORY

The **Tri-part Learning Story** is structured in **3 interlinking components**. This includes a learning episode, which is a succinct narrative of a learning engagement observed. It can also be the outline of a conversation with a child, a comment/decision or choice made by a child using the child's actual words or a comment made by a family member.

The **Learning Goals Achieved** *(summary of learning)* relates the story to the learning goals of the early childhood curriculum. This offers a summary of dispositions, skills, knowledge, attitudes and understanding **evident in the learning episode**.

The **'Help me build on this'** or 'Forward Plan' element of the learning story describes how the educator and parent can further build on the child's achievements and self-esteem. This can include pedagogical strategies, and/or resources and/or activities to be included in emergent planning.

This section can incorporate both **child and educator ideas** and should be shared with family in real-time to enable timely supports and positive reflection at home.

Educators use photographs, copies of children's work and comments from parents to support the written narrative.

*Captured on MOSAIC Educator, Aoife's story 'Fall Down' is a tri-part learning story with 3 components – the **learning episode, the learning observed including dispositions, and a forward plan**. The story records the time, and place and includes parent and educator engagement.*

*Learning goals and dispositions included are **relevant to, and visible within**, the learning episode. The forward plan is aimed at educators and family and will build on Aoife's developing language skills and self-confidence. Images add visual context to Aoife's story.*

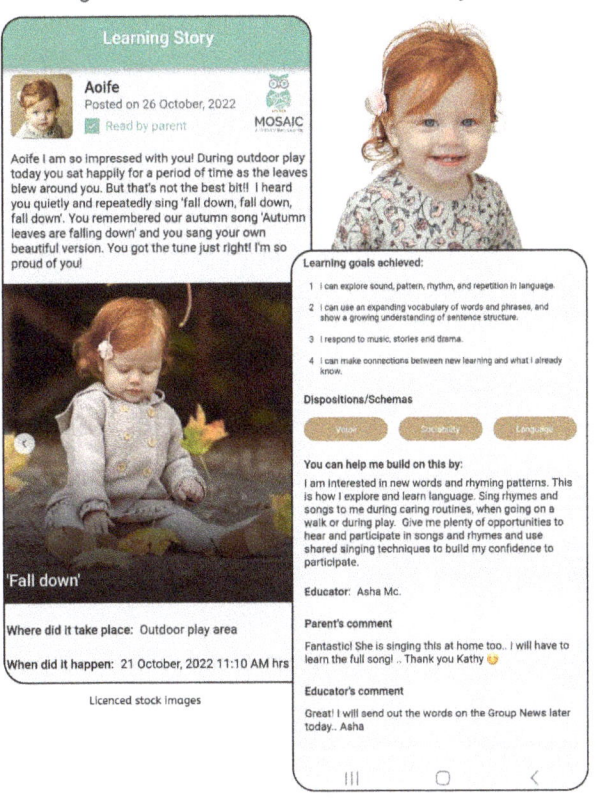

Captured on MOSAIC Educator, Freddie's story 'Fearless Freddie!', documents Freddie's actions while having fun outdoors on the swing. The educator uses the story to showcase **Freddie's developing dispositions** including confidence, risk taking and having fun. The educator then highlights some further strategies to progress this learning thereby using the story as an assessment for learning tools.

In this tri-part learning story, the **key components are clearly visible** – a visual image, the learning episode, the learning observed including dispositions, a forward plan and parent engagement.

TRI-PART LEARNING STORY

'Fearless Freddie'

Fearless Freddie!

Well Freddie, what fun we had on the swing today! This was the first time you tried out the toddler swing and I'm so proud of your bravery! You squealed with delight as I pushed you to and fro. You were able to move your body to make the swing go faster and held on tight to the bar.

You laughed loudly every time the swing came back to me and I pushed you again. You showed me that you could balance so well in the seat and you were so happy and confident.

When I (eventually) lifted you out, you clapped your hands with me to celebrate your bravery and fearless swinging!

Learning goals achieved:

1. I am making strong social attachments and developing warm and supportive relationships.
2. I am discovering, exploring and refining my gross and fine motor skills.
3. I feel good and am proud of my achievements.
4. I use a range of body movements, facial expressions, and early vocalisations such as babbling to show feelings and share information.
5. I enjoy challenge and can take risks.

Dispositions/Schemas

Confidence   Resilience   Having fun
Happy   Sociability   Risk taking

You can help me build on this by:

My confidence to try new things is definitely growing. I respond well to lots of expressive praise like clapping and hugging to celebrate my achievements.

Support me to try out other physical challenges outdoors like climbing and balancing. Give me lots of variety to test out what I can do. Having an adult to support me and celebrate my achievements is helping me develop the confidence to take risks and challenge myself further.

Educator: Asha Mc.

MOSAIC

Parent's comment

Aw, I loved reading this! Just look at his wee face 😍..thank you for sharing this special moment ..Mary x

Educator's comment

You are welcome Mary, he laughed so much 😊..A

'My View'

The **My View** learning story on MOSAIC foregrounds child participation and voice as part of the documentation process.

This story is crafted using a lovely combination of Partnership Voice, Verbal Voice and Interview Voice *(see Chapter 5: The Voice Box)* in one beautiful child centred story. Gentle, probing adult child engagement and co-facilitation is used to capture child thoughts, interests and wishes. The educator documents the child's responses exactly as expressed or spoken.

The unique and innovative design of 'My View' puts a spotlight on completely child-led engagement and documentation. 'My View' employs photovoice and discussion as a means for children to express and deepen their understanding of an issue, concern or idea.

The format of My View acts as a child participation tool that gives **'Space, Voice, Audience and Influence'** (Lundy 2007) to the child and their early childhood experiences. The inclusion of child assent/consent is also a powerful child rights feature of this story format.

My View stories are not just for children who use verbal modes of communication. The **expressions, vocalisations and gestures of babies** can be documented to bring meaning to the child's experience and inform the educator of choices and preferences *(See Freddie's View 'Snuggle Blanket)*.

Additionality is achieved through exposure to learning in relation to the meaningful use of digital technology in the early childhood setting.

Ade's View '**I bought it with my own money**' demonstrates why buying a lunch bag for school is important in his present **lived experience**. The educator will use this interaction to support Ade during the **transition period**.

'I bought it with my own money'

Date and time: 02 May, 2023 10:35 AM hrs

I took these pictures because...

Ade brought his new lunch bag to school today to show all his friends. This prompted a chat with Ade on his thoughts about starting school..

'I got a new Spiderman bag for my lunch. It's for going to school. Spiderman is my favourite. I got it with my own money.
My sister Nia is there and I want to play with her at lunchtime. I know what school looks like because I pick Nia up every day.

This makes me feel...

A SUITCASE FULL OF STORIES

In Macey's My View Story **'Can we wear wellies?'**, by taking time to engage with Macey in this way, the educator has enabled Macey to assert her preference for outdoor play. Macey widens this choice by including her friend and ensuring that they can wear wellies!

This type of engagement is a good example of the Lundy (2007) child-rights model of participation as it includes the **4 key components** that need to be in place.

In the example, Macey is given **space** to contribute, a voice to express her views and choices, audience where she is listened to and **influence** where her preferences are acted upon. Macey's consent is explained and included, and parent engagement is also visible.

MACEY'S VIEW
Can we wear wellies?

I took these pictures because...
'Wellies and suits are for outside to play – in mud sometimes'

This makes me feel...

I would like to... *read books outside with Casey – can we wear wellies?*

You can help me build on this by... When asked, I have my own ideas for play. Give me time and space to express my ideas and thoughts. Ask me what I would like to do. When I need a little help, provide some learning provocations to support my preference to play outdoors.

Child informed consent/assent... M

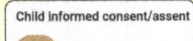

Educator: Catherine L.

MOSAIC

Comments:
Parent – This is great. She loves outside – the muddier the better! She spent some time with her Grandad in the garden on Saturday and loved it! Thank you for sharing – Laura x

Educator – I must mention that to her and find out more! – C.

A Picture Story

'Picture Story' is a quick and versatile mode of documentation. It can be used to send a quick update to family, as in the toddler example shown. Or it can capture a learning episode through a photograph or sequence of photographs.

Picture Stories enable the educator or child to capture an image of a piece of art so that the child's creation can be taken home in real time.

For children who can take the photograph themselves, this further involves the child in their own documentation process. Context can be added by adding a brief comment or description or the child's actual words used to add context to the Picture Story.

*CJ's Picture Story **'I'm doing great!'** acts a lovely connection with his mammy on his first day at creche. The story shows **time, people and place**. It only takes a few minutes to send, but from day one starts to establish **a meaningful connection** between the home and the early childhood setting. This story is infused with emotion - **empathy** for the parent, CJ's obvious **happiness** and the educator's **understanding** of what's important on a first day at creche.*

Today's children are digitally proficient and interaction with digital devices is not a new concept for many.

In this picture story, **'Tá mé Anseo' (I am here)**, and additional images, children use the MOSAIC Application to self-register each morning.

This encourages identity and belonging, independence, and technological empowerment.

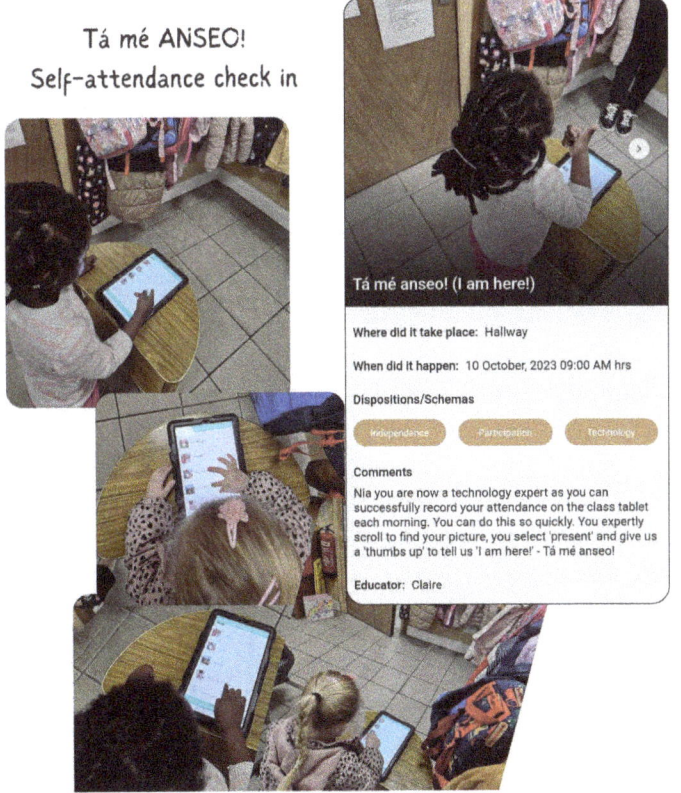

The use of technology in assessment has opened many new tools to the educator. Using video as a component of the documentation process offers educators **improved ways of observing children, storing and sharing information** about how a child **progresses over time**. 'Video Stories' can capture episodes like the child playing happily, a key learning moment, a conversation or group interactions. Video stories don't have to be long – a 30 second episode can demonstrate many dispositions, skills and attitudes during natural periods of play.

Observational assessment using video recordings offer a more authentic view of the child from a number of perspectives:
- A more **holistic image** of the child can be viewed and analysed - including **language, interactions and behaviour**.
- Video observations free up the educator from taking notes whilst observing - **the observation can be analysed later**.
- **Children can be involved** in replaying videos, reviewing and recalling learning. Viewing short video clips act as **meaningful reflections** of past group activities, events or projects when shown to children.

Videos are a useful instrument for **outside professionals** to be able to view the child during natural day to day experiences. This is useful to analyse holistic development including **language behaviour, and interactions** with a view to putting **support strategies** in place.

> *A short video story can capture the efforts of a toddler when facing the challenge of climbing the foam stairs. In 30 seconds, a video clip captures perseverance, balance and communication.*

The Snapshot Review

The **'Snapshot Review'** is a very flexible template with many uses. This template can provide a snapshot summary of the child's progress across different learning themes (for example, at Christmas). The review can take place to cover any time interval for example, the setting in period, each term or any interval deemed necessary by the educator/parent.

The Snapshot Review can also be used to provide a summary for in-service transitions (for example, from the baby room to the toddler room) as the report is succinct. It can also support a wider individual education plan or to document learning and development strategies and targets for a child who is neurodiverse.

Molly's Snapshot Review documents her settling in experience over the first 6 weeks of joining pre-school.

In this story, **'Will there be a farm at school',** Declan is keen to share this vital bit of information to inform advance preparation with his new teacher!

This 'My View' story created on MOSAIC Educator, demonstrates how child voice enriches the transition report to inform the new teacher about what is important to Declan in the transition process to school.

Declan's View

Will there be a farm at school?

Posted on: 26 May 2023

I took these pictures because... *'The farm is my favourite. Can you send these pictures to my new teacher?'*

This makes me feel...

I would like to... *'Tell my new teacher that I like the farm - will there be a farm at big school?'*

You can help me build on this by... Make sure to send this to my new teacher with my transition report. Mention that I have a keen interest in farm life and my favourite thing to do is to play with the animals, arrange them and share the all the things about animals that I already know.

Child informed consent/assent... **Declan**

Educator: EM

MOSAIC

Comments:

Parent – What a lovely story, I will pass on the farm information too!

Educator – Declan is most insistent that we pass this information on, so it all helps!

The Group Learning Story

The **Group Learning Story** can be used to capture either a collection of photographs taken during an outing or engagement with a particular activity or project.

The group learning story reflects the **interactions and learning of a group of children together**. A short description and learning dispositions portrayed can accompany the collection of images.

Group Learning Stories are a useful form of **evidence for emergent planning**. These stories can be filed with previous emergent plans to demonstrate learning in action. Group Learning Stories enable the educator to provide evidence of the entire group of children, actively engaging with the topic or interest on the corresponding curriculum plan.

Also, Group Learning Stories can be **displayed in floor books for the children to reflect on** or **use as provocations for discussion**. When displayed in hallways and corridors, this has the added benefit of **enabling families to view the activities of the group**.

The Group Learning Story ***'Can you make your own flower?'*** *on the next page, documents a creative learning provocation using natural flowers, petals, leaves and so on. The group activity involves a number of children who have free choice to design individual creations. A quick description of each image and positive learning dispositions observed add context to the story.*

Can you make your own flower?
Group Learning Story

MOSAIC

We used our senses to explore colour, smell and texture.

Interest - Exploration - Decision-making

We chatted, negotiated, shared resources and took turns using tools.

Communication - Problem solving - Respect

We made choices and created our own designs and patterns.

Creativity - Participation - Imagination

Building a story of learning for each child

Storybooks or Child Portfolios showcase the individual accomplishments and progress of each child.

In addition, the unique storybook will record when, where and how learning took place and who was involved in the learning episode. The portfolio can be a digital collection of stories, a physical portfolio, or a combination of both. Creating a tangible story of learning for each child will support learning outcomes, improve family involvement, and allow the educator to reflect on pedagogical practice and curriculum delivery.

It is important that educators are aware of not only the good practice guidelines around pedagogical documentation and assessment for learning, but also the documentation system used by the early childhood setting.

A **Curriculum Statement** and a **Documentation Policy** are required in this regard. The **Curriculum Statement** should provide a broad outline of the curriculum framework used including guiding principles, learning themes, learning goals and the type of activities on offer. This includes the documentation system used, recording expectations per child, and where support is available if necessary.

The pedagogical lead person has responsibility for ensuring that educators are supported and on track and cultivating an environment of sharing knowledge of individual processes to streamline the approach across the early childhood setting.

Digital and paper

Digital portfolios provide an electronic record of how a child progresses over time. This includes the electronic storage of learning stories, the child's work, as well as video and audio recordings of the child playing, talking and interacting. These are not only shareable with family, but with other professionals supporting the child.

A scrapbook of artefacts which is created by and accessible to children themselves is useful as a memory book. Digital storage does not have to replace this. However, the withholding of children's creations to add to paper portfolios or scrapbooks for giving to family as a keepsake at the end of a year is not ideal. Firstly, the child should have **ownership of their own work** by being able to share this with family when the interest or achievement is **'in the moment'**. Also, a child's family needs updates in real time to provide opportunities to build on learning interests at home, bolster confidence or celebrate the achievement. Holding paper documentation insights back for a later time in the year, creates missed opportunities to validate effort and build self-confidence.

Digital storybooks or portfolios offer many advantages. As all entries are dated automatically, a **timeline of progression** is recorded without effort by the educator. A significant advantage is the multi-modal nature of capturing information through audio, video and photography. Digital documentation offers a more **permanent and shareable** form of documentation which allows the child to take home authentic creative work in real time. Digitising some or all documentation portfolios makes them more accessible to family members and creates spontaneous opportunities for reflection at home.

Educator reflection

Storybooks of learning, or learning portfolios, are designed to show progression in learning so regular entries are necessary as goals and dispositions are achieved. Educators can reflect on their portfolio building using the following questions:

- Does each child portfolio receive the same attention?
- Is each child's portfolio different?
- Are entries dated and at regular date intervals?
- Are there a variety of story types (Picture/Video/Child Voice/Creative work)
- Is progression in learning visible?
- Is the child's individual interests visible through stories and images captured?
- Are there examples of the child's voice and decision making?
- Are family comments visible?

No one story format is more important than the other.

What is important is the ability of the story to connect educators and family for the benefit of the child.

A variety of story formats, modes of documentation, people and places are collectively used to build a relevant and progressive picture of the child as a learner.

This is multi-modal documentation.

CHAPTER 7
Pulling out the positives

A STORY OF LEARNING

As an adult, I'm now aware of how I work and learn best. My brain processes and retains imagery and colour much easier than any other medium. I'm creative and prefer quietness to work. This self-awareness helps me work to my maximum ability.

The same applies to children. I believe that an over-reliance on traditional 'academic' ability coupled with a 'one size fits all' approach, has thwarted the potential to see the child as an individual. This is why we must be gatekeepers of the child-led principles of early education.

This chapter considers a strength-based perspective where educator proficiency in responding to the child's personality, interests and preferred learning style will provide the optimal circumstances for learning. The role of meaningful documentation in highlighting and nurturing individual strengths, interests and preferences are demonstrated.

Start with strengths

The process of learning and development can vary greatly between children due to differences in the way they learn, as well as other factors, such as exposure, relationships, and life experience.

Children have distinct learning preferences in play, friendship, or environmental contexts.

For this reason, a one-size-fits-all approach to providing for children's learning is ineffective at best. And often severely detrimental to the learning process.

For some children, the way their brain is wired causes them to perceive and respond to things in unique ways. When educators are equipped to understand and embrace these distinctive characteristics, it not only helps children feel supported, but provides an opportunity to find innovative solutions to support learning. All children possess strengths that can be nurtured. We just need to take the time to recognise them and respond appropriately.

Using a strength-based approach, or **'pulling out the positives'**, is an effective pedagogical strategy to draw attention to and validate children's unique strengths. Children who are conscious of their strengths and how to apply them develop important self-awareness that they will use throughout life.

What is a strength-based approach?

The strength-based model is a **collective of pedagogical strategies** that educators use to demonstrate what works well for a child, what they know, and what they can do with support.

The strength-based perspective does not ignore challenge, rather it utilises the child's successes to support further learning and development. **This means that rather than trying to make every child fit the curriculum, the curriculum is built to respond to every child.**

The strength-based approach is underpinned by **children's rights, equity and participation**. That is, it's the child's right to participate from their own unique starting point in a way that best responds to who they are as a learner. The belief is that each child is capable and competent, possessing unique learning preferences, strengths and interests should be acknowledged as **positive contributors** to learning and development.

This strategy draws on individuality and uses **positives to nurture more positives**. For example, a child who displays anti-social behaviour will more readily respond to adult attention that is given to positive aspects of behaviour, no matter how minor. Or a child who may choose to play with the same resources over and over should be validated for their interest and progression. Provocations can be provided relating to the broad area of interest, instead of trying to change the child's preferred play choices.

Promoting a strength-based approach and sharing learning stories with family, the same supportive techniques to empower the child as a learner are utilised. This is particularly valuable for family who may not be familiar with strength-based techniques. Rather than receiving a discouraging list of 'deficits', they are encouraged to use **motivation and confidence building** with the child at home.

A combination of engagement strategies are used by the educator to facilitate strength-based engagement with babies, toddlers and young children.

Empowering techniques such as **meaningful praise and validation, scaffolding learning and co-constructing learning are all elements of a strength-based collective**.

Through an ongoing cycle of observation, documentation, planning and reflection, educators can identify the child's preferred learning style, what motivates them, their interests and capabilities.

Neurodiversity

Neurodiversity is the concept that there are naturally occurring differences in how a child's brain functions. It is not a giant leap to realise that this means that children who are neurodiverse learn differently. When a child thinks and learns differently, the focus should be on creating the circumstances in which they are enabled to participate and learn.

Whilst it's important to provide the necessary interventions and supports for challenges, it's helpful to consider the child's unique strengths in helping them find areas of competence. There is an onus on educators to ensure that they 'see' all children and understand 'how' they learn and 'what' supports they need.

Created on MOSAIC Educator, Tony's story 'Quiet Ears' documents how he is able to participate in outdoor play when he is provided with ear defenders to help him adjust to the raised noise levels outdoors. The short story also tells us that he finds the confidence to let go of the ear defenders and the educator after a short time.

The parent comment acknowledges the shared positivity about Tony's progress.

Where did it take place: Outdoors

When did it happen: 23 May, 2023 11:20 AM hrs

Dispositions/Schemas

Comments

Before going outside today, Tony asked for his 'quiet ears'- these help him enjoy outdoor play without being overwhelmed by all the loud noise. He played happily exploring and climbing on the tyres - occasionally checking that I was nearby. After 10 minutes of so, the 'quiet ears' (and me!) were disguarded when he found the confidence to join Kyle and Michael to take turns on the slide.

Educator: Teresa C.

Parent's comment

Differentiation –meeting the needs of the individual child

Curriculum differentiation is a broad term referring to the need to tailor learning environments and processes to create equitable learning experiences for all children.

Successful differentiation requires that educators value the achievements of all children and **recognise the right** of all children to be included while acknowledging that children learn in different ways. The main elements of differentiation include providing **content, processes and environments**.

- **Equitable learning content** - what children are learning - how appropriate is this to their individual needs, ability, lived experience, interests?

- **Equitable learning processes** - the strategies that work best for the child - what adaptations or communication strategies are required?

- **An equitable learning environment** - the suitability of the environment indoors and outdoors - how can this be arranged or adapted.

Educators provide differentiated opportunities by maintaining a positive, open mindset about possibilities for learning at all stages of children's development.

These attitudes are essential when working with all children, for example, 'typically' developing children, unusually able children, children with behavioural difficulties, children with different social, cultural, emotional and economic experiences, children with autism, children with dyslexia, children with visual, hearing and physical disabilities and children with language and developmental delay, including those children who have Down Syndrome.

In Niall's Learning Story - *'I'm not scared of worms any more'*, the educator skilfully encourages Niall's participation whilst respecting his individual learning pace. Positive interaction strategies such as **social praise, friend buddying and reflection** are used to scaffold Niall's continued ability to explore and get involved.

Supporting **positive dispositions to learn** are central to this learning story and the plan for progression at the end, coupled with the parent engagement will ensure that Niall continues to grow resilience, self-confidence and curiosity. Although the learning story focuses on Niall's progress, the **contextual supports** including his friend, the educator and the natural environment are clear.

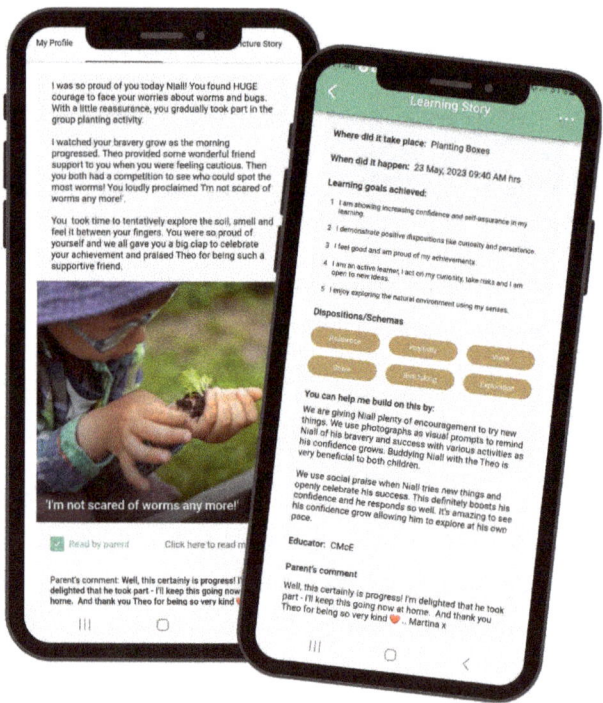

Recognising strengths and multiple abilities

Based on research from psychology, linguistics, neuroscience and other cognitive disciplines, multiple intelligences theory (Gardner, 1997) goes a long way in helping educators identify different modes of intelligence in babies, toddlers and young children.

Whilst not limiting the traditional learning abilities like mathematics and language as indicators of intelligence, the theory includes more diverse abilities, such as musical, emotional and nature-based skills. For example, the visual learner who can process information best when it can be seen, the kinaesthetic learner will prefer hands-on activities and the linguistic learner will learn through discussion and listening. Insight into how children present multiple strengths is fundamental to the educators understanding and practical implementation of **equitable** child-led learning.

Some strengths are obvious, and some are not so obvious.

This means that learning environments need to include opportunities for children to show what they know in multiple ways (i.e., by what they create, draw, say, and do). To enable children to make meaning through multiple forms of intelligence, children need to be able to engage in opportunities to use a variety of ways of knowing (e.g., linguistic, interpersonal, naturalistic and so on).

Educators can draw on multiple intelligence theory, as part of the strength-based approach to support children to learn by using their naturally preferred learning style and context as demonstrated in the graphic *'Children Are All Kinds of Smart'.*

Documenting strengths and dispositions

Documentation processes should not be confined to academic-led curriculum goals.

Thematic curriculum frameworks such as Aistear (2009) and Te Whāriki (2017) promote holistic learning processes through interconnecting learning themes, instilling value on unique strengths and positive dispositions to learn.

Ongoing documentation processes that focus on the **individual child** build capacity by allowing a more customised response. Child-focussed documentation, such as learning stories, which start with what the child **can do**, keep the spotlight firmly on the strengths of the individual child, **regardless of what these strengths may be**.

Whilst learning story documentation always starts with what the child can do, it is always important to support the child's specific learning needs by **linking** any further planned activities to the curriculum plan.

Starting with what is presently working for the child, and using strategies to support this, form the basis of any documentation/assessment about a child's progress in learning and development *(See Cillian's learning story, 'When Life gives you puddles- Jump!')*.

This means that the success of a child-led approach is largely dependent on the ethos of the early childhood setting, child-led documentation and educator insight to provide **content, processes, and environments** appropriate for every child.

Cillian's learning story 'When life gives you puddles- JUMP!' *demonstrates who Cillian is as a learner - a physical explorer who likes to engage with the natural environment to test his ideas and work things out. We can clearly identify his skills and strengths. The episode also prompts the educator to plan further activities that respond to Cillian's interests, preferences, abilities and needs.* **In relation to needs,** *the need to support language development and this is planned through activities that connect with Cillian's puddle experience.*

Your story..
Today Cillian you found yet another puddle and took the opportunity to explore. You very confidently walked straight into the puddle and laughed with delight as you got increasingly wet! You tried out some very impressive two legged jumps off the ground, some great hops and even a few skips!
You kicked the water using your right foot and swished the water with your right hand. You danced on the spot, stomped and tapped your feet in the water. You closely observed your feet as you made patterns in the water.

Your strengths and learning..
I can see wonderful positive dispositions such as confidence, curiosity, resilience and having fun. You are happy to try new things and take an opportunity when it presents itself. You showed me that you are happy to explore using your senses and to use your hands and feet to do this. You demonstrated fantastic balance and coordination as you negotiated the big puddle and moved your body in different ways.

How we will build on this..
Let's build on your interest in water by chatting about what else we can do. How about making tracks and patterns with your trike through water? Maybe you would like to manipulate objects in water - empty and fill, splash and pour, swish and move?

To support your growing language abilities, we will use your photographs to talk about and reflect on your puddle experience and use all the action words to describe your movements and skills. We will read the Peppa book 'The biggest muddy puddle in the world' and make meaningful connections to your own muddy puddle adventure.

Gruffalo Stories

The learning story extracts that follow were captured when Anna (the educator) used a favourite story 'The Gruffalo' during a small group activity with her key children in the pre-school room.

The story extracts featured here demonstrate how children's engagement with the Gruffalo story motivated **different play responses from three of the children**. The learning story examples show that each child adopted their own **unique play story** because of engaging with the story.

The educator ensured that the Gruffalo provocations like the book, figures and so on, were accessible in the environment in the days that followed. The educator then **watched and waited for the children's response**.

During the learning episodes that followed the storytelling activity, she skilfully engaged with each child. This was done by enabling them to take the **lead and use open questioning, expression, role play and validation** to understand the children's thought process in each documented play episode.

Documented on MOSAIC Educator, these stories provide a meaningful insight into what is important to each child at this time, what they are interested in, and the connection to their lived experience. This information will inform **child-led emergent curriculum planning**.

RIAN'S STORY: 'NEARER THE SKY FOR THE BIRDS TO SEE'

It is easy to see Rian's **naturalistic intelligence** and home background in his play episode influenced by the Gruffalo story. The **unique interest and lived experience** emerging from this episode is farming and animals.

He knowledgeably uses the information that he **already knows** (strength) about farming and applies this to make it **meaningful** to a new learning experience with his friend Aidan.

The writing perspective is that the educator '**tells the story**' to Rian, and includes Rian's own verbal voice to add authenticity to the story.

Rian took time to recreate his play story prompted by the Gruffalo story and in doing so, clearly demonstrates **positive dispositions like creativity, imagination, co-operation, decision making and purposefulness**.

Yesterday we read your favourite story 'The Gruffalo' together with Enya and Ade. Rian, you had great fun doing the Gruffalos very deep voice. You listened so well and knew the exact part of the story to use your big Gruff Gruffalo voice!

Today, I noticed you setting up the Gruffalo and some farm animals as you played on the grass with Aiden. You told me that the Gruffalo is going to live on the farm to 'scare all the birds away'..Gruffalo is very scary looking .. when the birds see his sharp claws, they will fly fast away again .. Aidan helped me'.

Rian you had the brilliant idea of placing the Gruffalo in your field and using him instead of a scarecrow. You put the Gruffalos arms up in the air - very scary!

When I asked why the scarecrow was up high, you said that you put the Gruffalo 'up the hill' and the other animals 'down in the field' 'because he is nearer the sky for the birds to see'.

ENYA'S STORY: 'DON'T BE SCARED ANNA'

We can see from Enya's story that she has strengths as a **strong communicator**. Her **linguistic and interpersonal intelligence** is used to negotiate a fun interaction with the educator and she uses the medium of drawing to **communicate** her thoughts.

The learning story is created by the educator using **partnership voice**, where Enya skilfully leads a two-way conversation, demonstrating positive dispositions such as **confidence, sociability and sense of humour**. A significant **emotional strength** displayed by Enya is her kindness and ability to reassure the educator.

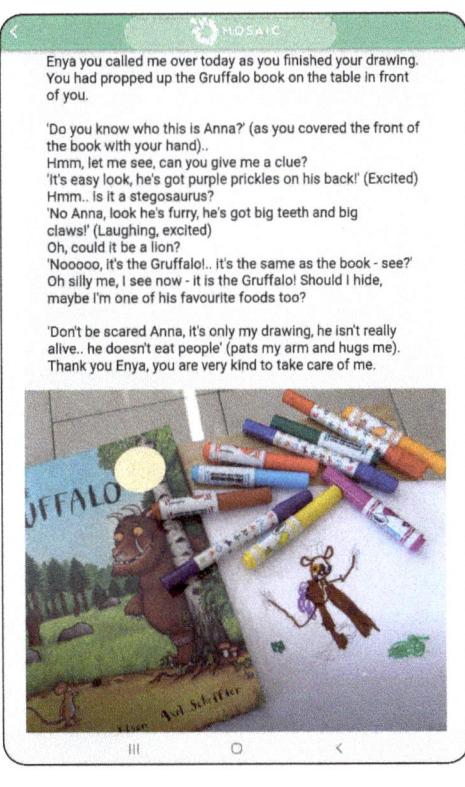

Enya you called me over today as you finished your drawing. You had propped up the Gruffalo book on the table in front of you.

'Do you know who this is Anna?' (as you covered the front of the book with your hand)..
Hmm, let me see, can you give me a clue?
'It's easy look, he's got purple prickles on his back!' (Excited)
Hmm.. is it a stegosaurus?
'No Anna, look he's furry, he's got big teeth and big claws!' (Laughing, excited)
Oh, could it be a lion?
'Nooooo, it's the Gruffalo!.. it's the same as the book - see?'
Oh silly me, I see now - it is the Gruffalo! Should I hide, maybe I'm one of his favourite foods too?

'Don't be scared Anna, it's only my drawing, he isn't really alive.. he doesn't eat people' (pats my arm and hugs me).
Thank you Enya, you are very kind to take care of me.

ADE'S STORY: 'MY MOSAIC'

Ade's interest and skill in using technology is demonstrating his **spatial and visual intelligence**. It also shows his understanding the **connectedness ability of technology** to share something important to him with his mammy.

He uses his **verbal voice** to get the educator to respond to his idea and demonstrates dispositions of **decision making, motivation and independence**.

Engagement and interaction strategies such as **open-ended questioning and validation** utilised by the educator as part of this partnership voice learning story.

Today you were on the floor looking at the pictures in the Gruffalo book and carefully holding the soft Gruffalo. You observed me closely as I made some notes on my tablet.

'Can I send a picture of the Gruffalo to mammy's phone?'
Sure, but how can we do that?
'You go here' (selecting camera icon on the tablet) 'and then press this circle here'..
'Can you put it on my Mosaic and mammy will see it?'
Fantastic idea, let's do that.
'Let's go outside because the Gruffalo lives outside'.

You very carefully positioned the Gruffalo and the book by the hedge. You purposefully set up your picture just as you wanted it. You took a number of photos but chose this one to send to your mammy. Ade you are a very creative photographer!

Same experience, different responses

The way that these three children have experienced the **same Gruffalo story activity**, and initiated **three unique responses**, is both fascinating and revealing. It also reaffirms the importance of tuning-in to the child as an individual and providing the **time and space to reflect and recreate experiences**.

Each child took the provocation offered by the Gruffalo story and used it to **shape their play response** drawing on their **unique strengths, what they already know/can do using their preferred learning style**. The learning episodes show the richness of children's imagination, how they can make activities meaningful to them, their thought process and level of understanding.

By creating three child-focussed learning stories, the educator demonstrates respect for the **thought processes, interests and responses of each child**. These unique insights will inform the next steps for each child, positioning them at the centre of **child-inspired practice**.

Rather than trying to make every child fit a curriculum, the curriculum should be built to respond to the uniqueness of every child.

CHAPTER 8
Revisit, recall and reimagine

A STORY OF LEARNING

The documentation portfolio, whether digital or paper-based, should be viewed as the child's property, with educator responsibility, family engagement and professional oversight – in that order. The ownership and purpose of documentation strongly reflect the ethos and child-led value system of the early childhood setting.

This chapter underlines the necessity of meaningful engagement in the documentation process on behalf of the child, the educator and the family and highlights why documentation, especially dynamic digital systems, have much to offer children by revisiting learning, recalling experiences, and reimagining outcomes.

The importance of 'TIME'

The most valuable commodity in early education is time. When the baby, toddler or young child is given time to revisit activities, the neural pathways associated with specific skills or knowledge are strengthened. The process also transfers information from short-term to long-term memory. This improves **retention and recall of learning over time**.

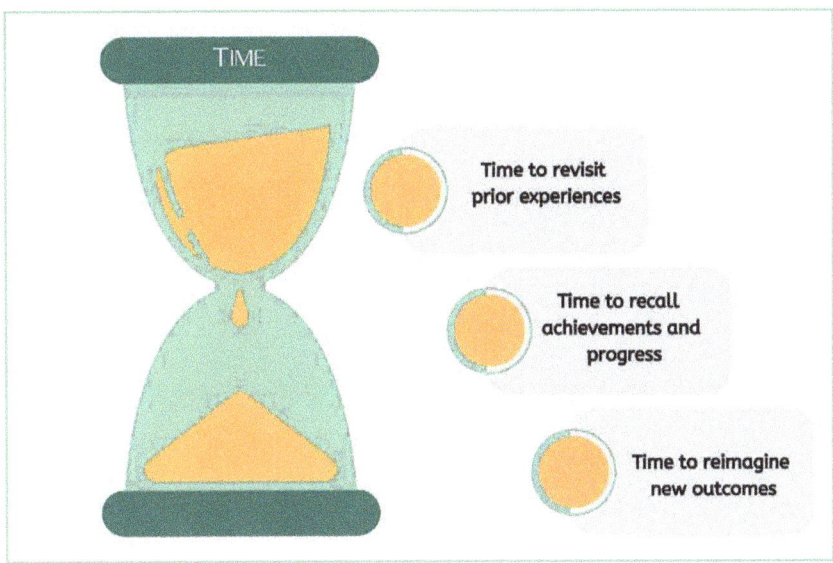

Repeatedly engaging in the same activities boosts children's confidence and self-esteem.

As they engage with a previous experience, resources and processes are familiar, allowing them to explore concepts in a more in-depth way. They can make connections, remember, and engage in meaningful discussions. This **builds mastery and deeper understanding**.

Documentation itself can assist this process. Therefore, documentation is not confined to the role of the educator and requires ongoing engagement and participation from children and family.

1. Engaging children

Children should play an active role in the documentation process. Not just as observers of a portfolio prepared by the educator, but as a regular contributor, creating content, choosing what to include, and **giving consent for sharing images**. The child's voice, choices and self-reflection should be ongoing in the documentation process.

Closely linked to this is the need to allow the child time. Pedagogical documentation is the embodiment of 'slow pedagogy' (Clark 2020). Time to revisit prior experiences. **Time to recall achievements and progress. Time to reimagine new outcomes.**

Children observe too

Babies, toddlers and young children observe too. They use observations of their surroundings, peers and familiar adults to orient themselves. This allows children to draw on things that are familiar, to feel secure and that they belong.

Involving children in the assessment and reflection process propels child participation to another level. By giving children **time** to define and analyse their own learning experiences, supports their working conceptions about how learning happens. Educators should commit to including children in both **self-evaluation** and **peer evaluation**.

In this context, documentation displays in the form of 'Living Walls' or 'What we know about...' displays and shared floor books, act as an accessible **visual spark** for memories and conversations. (See overleaf).

When a display is more than a display

Whilst simple labels for displays of children's work are useful, more detailed engagement with documentation helps educators to reflect more deeply on the relationships between pedagogical practice and how children learn. As well as providing evidence of learning and development goals, displayed documentation provides a visual stimulus for individual and group reflection.

This is not a once-off project, rather it is an ongoing **visual representation of everyday learning** in the child's environment. Once displayed or made accessible to children, past learning then has the potential to **ignite further learning**.

When educators thoughtfully display children's work or past activities, it creates a visual dialogue that can be tapped into at any time. In addition to affirming and validating a child's work, voice and ideas, this practice promotes higher level thinking, metacognition and reflection.

Educators who know how to **'use documentation'** allows the child to make a connection to the initial experience. Regardless of their age or ability, this allows children to revisit, recall and reimagine. Through these participative processes, children become active contributors to the documentation and assessment process.

Images courtesy of Little Stars Pre-school, Moville, Co. Donegal

This display of imagery from the 'Spa Day' when displayed on the wall will provoke many conversations and memories.

- **Can you remember** what the bubbles felt like on your toes?
- **Who** owns those feet?
- **What** was your favourite spa snack?
- **How** did we make the lemonade - can you remember the ingredients?
- **Should we** have another spa day - what else can we plan to do?

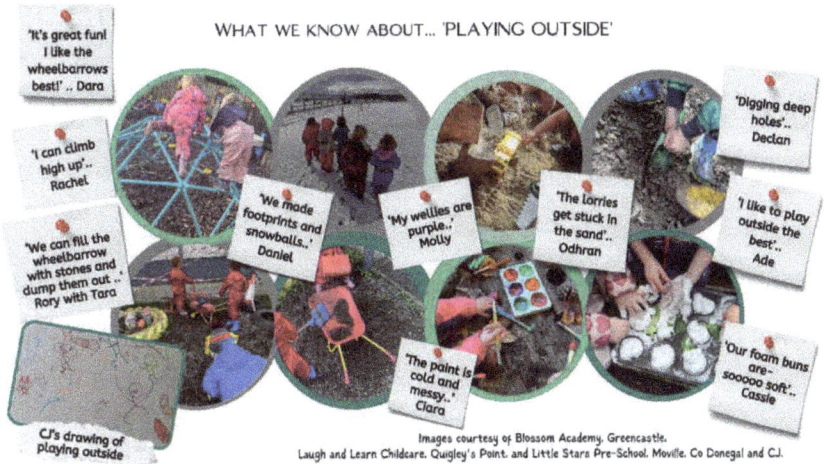

Images courtesy of Blossom Academy, Greencastle. Laugh and Learn Childcare, Quigley's Point, and Little Stars Pre-School, Moville, Co Donegal and CJ.

'Living Wall' documentation

- **'What we know about..'** topics are an excellent way to enable children to **revisit and build** on what they know over a period of time as knowledge grows and becomes more in-depth. 'What we know about..' topics can provide a focus on anything of interest to children. In the example above *'What we know about .. Playing Outside'* educators have taken a topic that is meaningful to all children. It is meaningful because all children can identify with playing outdoors as it is part of their daily experience at home and in the early childhood setting.

- This type of participatory documentation allows educators to give **space and voice** to children's thoughts and ideas on different topics over a longer period of time - sometimes months. The growing wall display acts as a **'living wall'** and can typically include **photographs and drawings, artefacts, children's transcribed comments or conversations, and reflective educator comments**.

- **The living wall provides an excellent provocation to discuss new ideas or reflect on prior learning.** Children's observations and interests can be added on an ongoing basis, ensuring that ideas have audience and influence regarding their preferences and choices.

- Educators can choose topics on just about anything that is **meaningful to children**. For example, *What we know about.. family; our village/town/county; our body; leaves/trees/flowers; pets; recycling, or exercise.* Topics for babies and toddlers could include *What we know about.. our senses; mirrors and lights; circles; moving our bodies; messy things; schemas,* and so on.

Involving children in the documentation process

Children should feel a sense of agency and ownership over their visual record of achievements and progress. There are a number of practical ways in which this can be achieved, usually between a key person and a child or small group of children.

- Encourage children to document their work by taking photographs or narrating a short video to explain their work.

- Discuss with children what pieces of work they would like to include. For babies and toddlers, use simple 'Which one?' choice games to do this.

- Ask children's consent to use photographs that they themselves feature in.

- When documenting the 'Help me build on this section of a learning story – ask children where they would like to go next with this interest or activity.

- In one to one or small group work, allow time for children to self-reflect on their portfolio. This will allow babies, toddlers and young children to connect prior and new learning experiences, use memory and recall and most importantly, celebrate progress in learning and build a positive self-image as a learner.
- Group reflective discussions can also be facilitated by using Floor books containing group learning stories and photographs or photo slideshows to reflect on an outing or project. Positivity is further strengthened when this process is facilitated by parents and family.

*Ella replaying a short video which is part of her MOSAIC digital storybook. By **revisiting** the fun activity of mask making, Ella recalls the fun activity and the people involved. This provides a meaningful mechanism for **self-reflection** and for **sharing** this important experience with family.

The advantages of digital documentation for engagement

The **real-time connectedness** between the early childhood setting and family is one of the significant advantages of digital documentation. Family can be informed about emerging interests and learning experiences as they happen. This means that the child's experiences can be **discussed, consolidated and reflected** upon at home.

The multi-modality of digital documentation makes learning **vibrant and visible** for children and families through the combined modes of photographs, video, audio and narrative. From the child's perspective, this practice demonstrates the connected nature of the family-early childhood setting partnership and promotes a sense of belonging to both spaces. This does much to strengthen children's emotional well-being and self-esteem due to the value placed on their achievements.

For the educator, digital documentation lends itself well to situations where children, by their very nature and preferred learning style, appear more difficult to observe than others. For example, the child who builds constructions, paints pictures and can hold a conversation will always be a more ready subject for a learning story than a child who spends significant time playing alone or prefers not 'make' things. Educators may also find it more difficult to create stories of learning for children who use physical modes of communication, for example, through gestures, movement or gaze.

Video documentation

This is where the video mode of documentation can be very useful. Reviewing short video clips enables the educator to **'slow down' the observation** and look at babies, toddlers and young children and their behaviours in **greater detail.**

If documentation is to be fully equitable and consistent regardless of the child's individual characteristics, educators must be able to recognise the **subtle signs of learning** so that they can be supported and built upon. For example, the baby who looks intently at shadows and movement on a wall, gazing for a period of time is **equally valid** to a toddler or who concentrates for a period of time when using loose parts.

The learning **'hook'** is the child's ability to observe, to concentrate and think using a medium that interests them. Research shows that children's meaning making goes far beyond speech, and is expressed in complex combinations of movement, gesture, gaze, facial expression, images and manipulations of objects (Bezemer and Kress 2016). Meaningful learning stories can be created from either scenario once the educator knows what to look for.

The flexibility of digital documentation

Digital documentation, consultation and reflection with children is part of daily activities at this early childhood centre.

By documenting and discussing discoveries **'in the moment'** children can be involved in the process and share experiences with family in real time.

This not only gives children exposure to the meaningful use of digital technology, but this type of activity also allows children to have ownership over their own story and share key achievements with peers.

A 10-month-old baby reacts positively on seeing a video of himself on his MOSAIC storybook.

The educator uses this one-to-one engagement and interaction to look at pictures that the baby recognises. The educator reflects on the images with the baby, using interesting language and sounds to promote cognitive connections.

2. Connecting and engaging with family

The engagement of family in early education is a fluid and essential partnership between families and educators that plays a decisive role in shaping the child's educational journey. Central to this is regular and meaningful **communication, information sharing and respect** between family and educators.

Supporting family engagement

To enable family to engage with their child's learning and development, documentation updates should be **regular, accessible and communicated in real time.**

To ensure a high instance of parental engagement with documentation practices, the policy and expectations of this process need to be clearly communicated to family on enrolment of their child in the early childhood setting. In doing this, the early childhood setting should be cognisant of disparity of language, literacy capacity and availability of digital devices where appropriate. This includes:

- The broad objectives of the curriculum followed in the early childhood setting.
- The documentation system and communication system used – the rationale for this and any permissions needed.
- The type of information shared (learning stories, photographs, messages, news, reports etc) and how often to expect updates.
- Expectations for family contribution (comments in learning stories etc).
- How to access the digital documentation system (for example, the app stores or log in credentials).

An inter-reliant flow of encouragement

Educators spend considerable time and effort documenting children's ideas, interests and engagement to support children to reach the next stage in learning. These outcomes are further enriched when family are actively involved in the process. This is achieved through an **inter-reliant flow of encouragement** *(see graphic below)* that benefits the child, the educator and the parent.

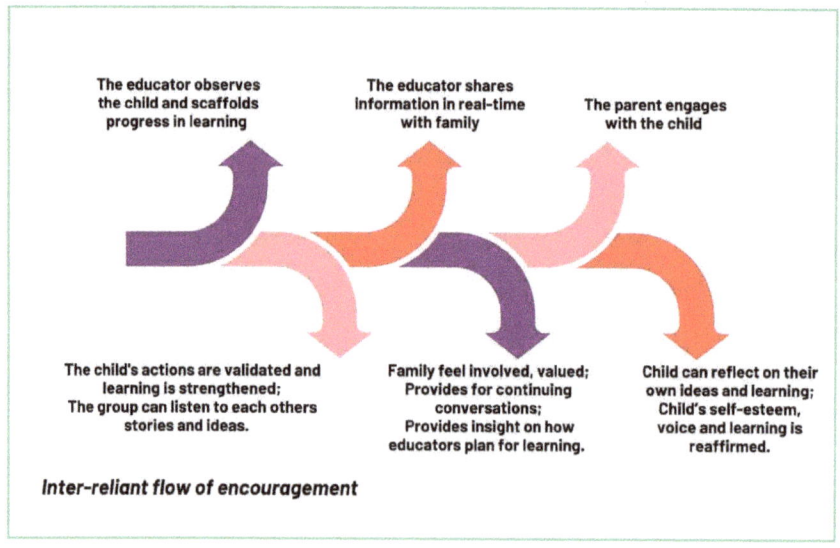

Inter-reliant flow of encouragement

Flow begins as the educator listens-in to babies, toddlers and young children and scaffolds progress in learning. Children's actions are validated and learning is strengthened in an individual and group context.

When the educator shares learning stories with family in real time, family feel involved and valued and have an important insight into how educators are working with their child, this provides a basis for continuing conversations between educator and family.

The flow is continued at home when family engages with the child. The child has an opportunity to reflect on their choices and achievements and experience a sense of **connectedness** between key adults in their lives currently.

Engaging family with learning stories

10 Tips for Educators

To maximise engagement with family, learning stories need to be engaging, individual to the child, jargon free and informative. Following are some practical tips for educators to make learning stories appealing to family.

1. Create a unique title
   Grab their attention. Draw family in. Educators want family to read the story. Make them want to read on. A unique title should be personal to the child, relate to the learning story or represent the child's exact words. When writing learning stories, the title doesn't have to come first. Once the pictures and text are assembled, the title often leaps off the page.

2. Make learning stories personal
   Every child shows interest in different things at different stages. Babies have their own interests and preferences. Toddlers may be working through a schema. And or young children may share little anecdotes about family life, pets and things that they like. Closely observing and listening-in is key, and for educators, allowing time to stand back and observe, provides many opportunities to create learning stories unique to the child.

   The most effective learning stories are ones that make family feel that the educator understands their child. There is no more powerful comment from a parent to an educator than – *'You know him so well!'* or, *'You have captured her perfectly!'*.

   Draw on what is already known about the child and family. Having regular conversations with children and family is helpful to discover what's happening at home, interests which will weave themselves into your observations and stories. For example, *'Jack is very keen to take his picture home to show his Grandad as we always hear great stories about Granda's dogs'.* or *'Friday is definitely a special day for Maura when Nana collects her from creche – she is always so excited to see Nana in the hallway'.*

   These types of comments, weaved into your stories or comments, highlight that you know the child and their routine, you listen to what they have to say, and that you value the stories shared.

3. Choose photos that tell a story
   A photograph can speak without words. Busy parents or parents who use a different first language, will look at photographs first, so it is important to choose photographs that 'speak' or tell a story.

'They grew into pears because we watered them'

Today Oisín, when exploring in the garden, you discovered that fruit had grown on our fruit trees during the summer holidays!

'Look, I can see pears on the trees - they are growing! ..Look everyone- look! Come on everybody, look at the pears.. and all the apples!'

Soon your friends Matt and Cassie had joined in. You were able to reach up and pick a pear from the tree and examined it closely in your hands. You told us 'they grew into apples because we watered them'.

You successfully used the school camera to take beautiful photographs of our fruit to add to your Mosaic.

Interest   Communication   Investigating

You can help me build on this by:
Oisín I asked you what we should do with our fruit. You suggested that we 'wash them in a basin to get all the dirt off.. and taste them'. You specified that we would have to 'take the skins off' as you 'don't like bumpy skins'.

So that's a plan, let's do some washing and cutting and tasting to see what happens! We will also see if we can find seeds to look at under the microscope and replant. We will also add your photos to your Mosaic so that you can show to your family and tell them all about your exciting discovery in the garden!

Learning goals achieved:

1 I am a capable, active learner.
2 I can speak confidently to give and receive information.
3 I can use books and ICT (camera, computer, tablet, headphones) for enjoyment and as a source of information.
4 I enjoy exploring the natural environment using my senses.
5 I am beginning to develop my own ideas about why and how things happen.

Educator: KMcP

Parent's comment
We heard about the apple trees today after preschool, great excitement 😊. We had to send granny the pictures and apparently we have to plant a pear tree!!

Created on MOSAIC Educator, Oisín's learning story 'They grew into pears because we watered them' demonstrates the continuation of the story with family. Oisín's story seamlessly connects with parents and grandparents made possible by the real-time digital sharing of the story.

To support this, ensure selected photographs can act as a springboard for meaningful conversations with family. Remember, not every story needs detailed observations. A picture or video combined with a brief comment or caption will relay the story you want to tell if chosen carefully.

4. Include the child's voice as much as possible
   Including the child's voice in learning stories is a lovely way of authentically sharing exactly what the child said or expressed using different modes of communication.

For example, educators can weave a child's exact words into a learning story or use the child's words to describe a piece of art or construction. When using a child's actual words, do not correct the child's grammar when transcribing the story– **relay the child voice as spoken**. When interpreting expressions or gestures, keep comments age appropriate and as authentic as possible.

In the Picture Story example 'My Geansaí is green', the educator adds the child's explanation of the drawing using his exact words as spoken.

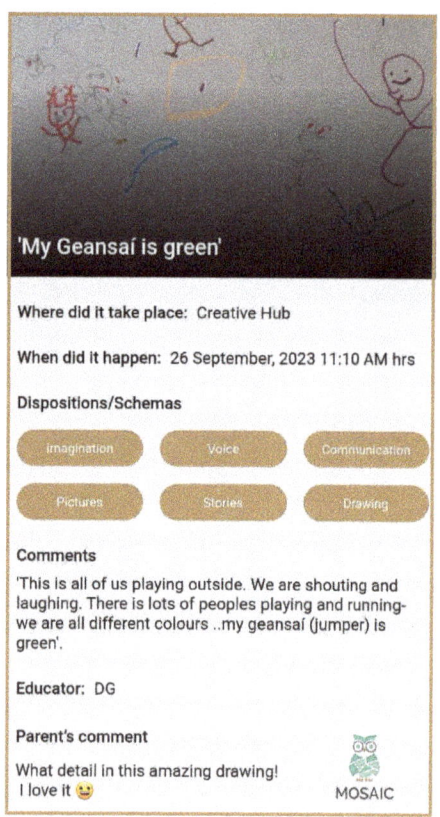

5. Educators craft the story

In the main, the educator crafts the learning story. The educator draws on humour, love, professional language, strength-based perspectives and appreciation of how young children learn.

It should be possible to feel a passion for early education and the educators **enthusiasm and pride** in the child's learning growth being described. This will make the story come alive for family.

6. Prompt engagement

Invite family to engage with learning stories shared by adding a quick comment. Family may need repeated encouragement to do this – share positive messages inviting them to comment, thank them when they do comment and **keep communication regular and flowing**.

The forward planning section of a learning story is an ideal way to involve parents to reinforce learning at home. When the 'forward planning' component of the learning story is framed from the perspective of what the child needs to further develop learning, family can see their role in making this happen at home too.

7. The importance of real- time!

For documentation to be used to its full potential for learning, it needs to be done regularly and consistently. Keep the child's storybook/portfolio current and up to date by adding quick picture stories and child voice snippets.

Of course, this practice is largely meaningless if it is not shared with family in real-time. Learning stories or updates shared months after they have taken place, loses the critical learning period captured in the documented story and bypasses meaningful learning partnerships with family.

Digital documentation enables the child to have **ownership of their own work** in the moment, to bring treasured artwork home in real-time – rather than storing it away in a scrapbook until the end of the year. By using a photograph of the artwork in the digital portfolio, the child can bring the creation home which allows for real-time discussion, acknowledgement of achievements and confidence building.

When learning stories are shared with family in real-time, the child's learning interest is still current and in the moment. This means that parents are more likely to engage with the child, supporting the child's interests and reinforcing learning in the home environment. This dual approach to in the moment learning, serves to strengthen the learning experience, building child confidence and self-esteem.

8. Avoid gaps

   Avoid long gaps in communication. To ensure that family consider the partnership between the early childhood setting and home as an ongoing cycle of communication, ensure that **updates are regular**. This does not always have to be a learning story, it could be a picture added to the child's gallery, a short video or a group news update.

9. Display project work or create 'Living Walls' for ongoing updates

   Use areas where family gather or pass through to display project work. Avoid displaying all documentation within the classroom. It makes sense to also use outdoor notice boards, hallways and entrance areas.

10. Use quick group news updates

Quick news updates for all parents at once as a quick way of keeping parents informed and keeping your communication system engaging. See the examples below from MOSAIC Educator.

Stories of digital connectivity

One of the often-overlooked advantages of digital documentation is its ability to enable the connectivity of children with family all over the world. To highlight this, on the next page are 2 stories from an early childhood setting in County Donegal who use MOSAIC Educator and MOSAIC Family as their documentation and communication system for each child.

STORY 1

*Yana came to Ireland from Ukraine. Her son has just started his 2nd Preschool year in a preschool in County Donegal. This is Yana's story of connection in her own words..

'I like it so much this application, share it with family, they see he's playing here and how he's happy and has friends. To grandpa in Ukraine, sister in Ukraine. Dad in Ukraine, working in Ukraine, he observe and see, they enjoy to see him. I translate the learning stories and send them so more relatives, family can see. They (the preschool) have lots of costumes get gifts, relatives happy to see he has a great time here playing outside. Because it is different here, we don't celebrate Halloween and Easter is different, no hunt, no chocolate eggs just real ones, paint them. In Ukraine use Viber, WhatsApp to share for parents - it's not individual like this'.

STORY 2

*Maria originates from Brazil. Her 4 year old son *Noah attends Pre-School in County Donegal. Maria has close and extended family in Brazil, in Kenya and in Ireland. This is Maria's story of connection in her own words..

'The Mosaic App has enabled my family in Brazil, Kenya and Ireland to follow the development, activities and memorable moments that my 4-year-old son has at play school by reading the feedback of his teachers and looking at pictures and videos the teachers post of him. It also gives me the chance to get to know the funny stories he tells his teachers and classmates. It's a great way to get to know more about my son through his interaction with other people, showed on this app. This app is simply fantastic'.

*not real names

CHAPTER 9
Why predict the unpredictable?

A STORY OF LEARNING

It can be all too easy to fall into the habit of planning predictable curriculum themes year after year. Despite the learning opportunities that seasonal and celebration themes can present, without blending child interests and needs with the theme, activities may not interest all children and can inhibit them from following their own natural learning interests.

Some seasonal themes can be over reliant on creative activities, meaning that other areas of learning may be overlooked. This can mean that the plan is not balanced in terms of holistic learning. From the educator perspective, repeated themes can become monotonous where it may be difficult to feel enthused and excited by a particular topic, if repeated without change, on a continuous basis.

This chapter considers emergent, child-inspired planning where children's interests add an important dynamic to curriculum planning, where the only thing that is predictable is the unpredictable.

Child inspired practice

An emergent approach to curriculum is easy to spot. Educators are proactive in making informed decisions in response to children's well-being, interests and learning needs.

Educators can be heard engaging with babies, toddlers and young children by validating their vocalisations, gestures and play choices. There is a repartee of discussion, open-ended questioning, meaningful praise and validation for children's ideas and contributions. The environment is full of open-ended resources and play provocations are part of the everyday set up. Creative displays and children's work may not be perfect in the representational sense, **but they will be perfect in the individual sense.**

Emergent curriculum is based on a **child-led approach** where children learn best when experiences represent their interests, preferences, abilities and needs. Children's interests sparked through play or lived experience are a springboard for planned learning activities – creating an emergent **curriculum of play**. This means that the curriculum 'emerges' and meaningful learning experiences make up the curriculum plan.

Common misconceptions

A common misconception about emergent curriculum is that it has to be completely child initiated.

This is not the case. Emergent curriculum uses both child and educator input as a starting point for planning learning experiences. At times, topics emerge from the interests of babies, toddlers and young children. Maybe a young child recently visited a travelling circus and saw elephants, or discovered a spider in the car and now their **interest is sparked**. A baby may have noticed lights on the ceiling or a toddler may be fascinated with objects that spin. Regardless of the child's age or ability, an interest has emerged and they are **excited about it, interested in finding out more and motivated to learn**.

By way of framing children's interests under the curriculum framework, educators will introduce **topic scaffolds** or prompts to support children's learning and development. Executed through the resources available in the outdoor and indoor environment, this **mutual negotiation** between what is **of interest to the child and what the educator knows, is a powerful dynamic for holistic learning and development**.

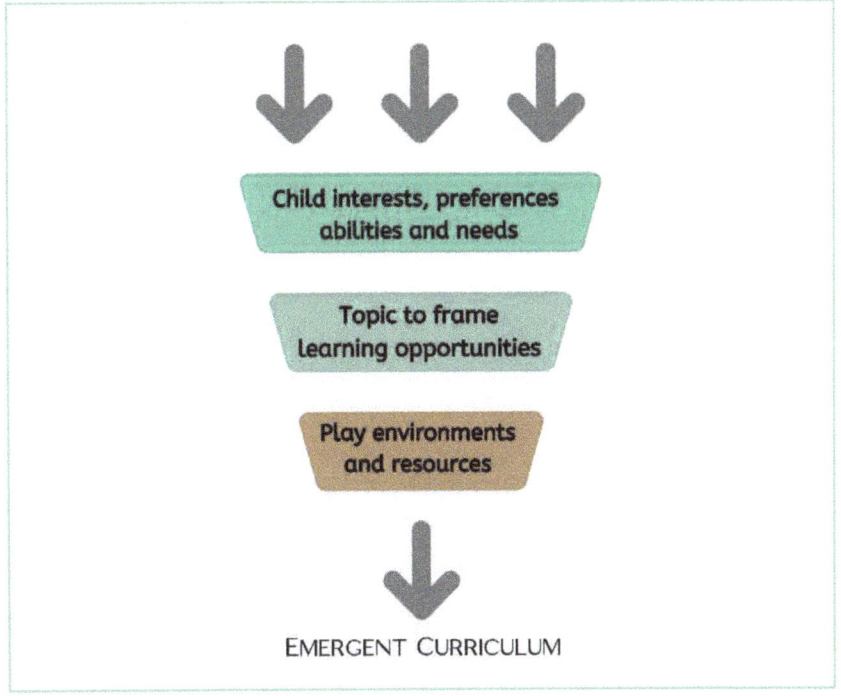

Educators committed to this teaching philosophy use observations, discussions and the observed play behaviour of children to gather information to construct curriculum content. Meaningful learning opportunities are arranged on a curriculum plan framed by curriculum theme headings.

As children grasp skills and dispositions over time, educators respond by enriching the learning experience by planning and offering increasingly challenging tasks. As children repeatedly confront and master these self-led challenges, they come to view themselves as **competent, validated learners.**

The proficient educator

Educators play a crucial role in their commitment to the implementation of emergent curriculum.

Using knowledge of child development theory, pedagogical strategies and the individual child, they make available an enabling environment of spaces and resources, for children to actively explore and learn.

Since learning requires repeated practice by the child, these interests are sustained through the continued cycle of **listening-in and observing, documenting and analysing, planning and implementing and reflecting and evaluating.**

This cycle is designed to enable each child in a manner that is mindful of individual ability. Once a skill/learning has been achieved, learning interests are enriched through the addition of new materials that prompt or support new ideas. At this stage, the educator **scaffolds and connects the child's interests and play experiences** to bring them to a new level of understanding/ability.

In addition to providing ongoing opportunities for play-based exploration across the curriculum, planning for emergent curriculum requires educators to **document and capture learning as it unfolds**.

Documenting learning experiences helps educators understand children's engagement with learning and inspires ideas for where the curriculum might go next. It also helps children remember and understand the process of their own learning and gives parents concrete representations of their children's developmental growth.

Emergent curriculum does not magically happen. It requires that educators actively seek out and plan for the interests of the child. This kind of pedagogical practice values the child as a unique individual with a voice and a right to participate.

Using 'Invitations to Play' and 'Play Provocations'

We all need a little motivation to try something new!

In relation to inquiry-based learning in early childhood education, the terms **'invitations to play'** and **'play provocations'** are used as part of the pedagogical approach to emergent curriculum. They are applied interchangeably to suggest prompting curiosity and exploration through play. There is however, a subtle difference between the two ideas.

'Invitations to Play' and 'Play Provocations' – what's the difference?

- An 'invitation to play' can be described as **mindfully planned spaces** that encourages exploration, engagement and discovery.

- A 'play provocation' is **an activity framed by a broad idea** that provokes action and stimulates thinking.

What does an invitation to play look like?

An 'invitation to play' is how educators create interesting and responsive play environments for children.

This can be achieved through mindfully planned spaces indoors and outdoors, including hidey spaces, accessible loose parts, real life artefacts, challenging physical equipment, and creative materials - to name but a few. Providing an environment full of invitations to play is a very simple yet effective way to 'open the door' to children to explore and investigate different open-ended materials, resources and spaces.

Invitations to play act as a prompt to the child to follow their interests, provoke thinking and nurture creativity. See samples of open-ended invitations to play in the image below.

Setting up invitations to play

There are no rules about invitations to play. The way educators set up the play environment draws on a number of areas. For example, educators may have broad learning outcomes in mind as they set up play invitations in the environment or they could be created in response to a child's interest. Other educators favour mainly natural resources and outdoor exploration when creating an environment full of invitations to play. A balanced blend of all is a productive approach.

What does a play provocation look like?

Provocations are a pedagogical strategy used to spark inquiry and thought processes.

Provocations are a collective of materials or objects set up for the child with a **broad idea behind the collective**. Materials and objects used should be open ended and non-gender specific. They should not intrude on the child's freedom to play, imagine or create.

Provocations provide a stimulus to provoke thought and ideas encouraging creativity, decision making and independence. As learning has no specific goals, children can follow their own thought process and gain a sense of control and decision making. See an example of a documented play provocation below **'Can you make Awesome Autumn Soup'.**

The role of documentation in the planning cycle

Educators use documentation to show evidence of the planning cycle and to create visual recall stimulation for children. Understanding the purpose behind the planning cycle gives educators a solid foundation from which to grow professional documentation skills and to support the overall development of each individual child.

The planning cycle has several functions for pedagogical practice. It helps educators to engage with the curriculum framework used and plan experiences tailored to the interests, preferences, abilities and needs of the individual child.

Educators reflect on the effectiveness of practice and experiences and set goals and targets for **individual and group learning**. Engaging with the planning cycle in collaboration with colleagues and team members, ensures that educators share useful information and work on a consistent approach.

The planning cycle

The planning cycle designed to enable the learning and development of babies, toddlers and young children, can be divided into 4 stages:

1. Listen-in and Observe.
2. Document and Analyse.
3. Plan and Implement.
4. Reflect and Evaluate.

A SUITCASE FULL OF STORIES

Learning Story

Fantastic dancing today Louis, when your favourite song 'Happy Place' came on, you confidently sprang into action and twisted, waved your arms and sang in time to the music.

2 — DOCUMENT AND ANALYSE

You can help me build on this by:
My physical skills are developing so I need lots of opportunities to practice different movements using my whole body. Use my interest in music to play games such as Musical Chairs and Hopping Bunnies. Expose me to different types of music e.g. soft music, classical music and observe my reactions.

Educator: AC

1 — NOTICE THE INTEREST

6.11.23
Lewis: music, dancing

Dance like no one is watching

Parent's comment
Louis loves to dance, he dances with his big sisters at home too. Thank you, this is lovely .. Marion x

Where did it take place: Toddler room

Educator's comment
I know, we were very impressed!

When did it happen: 07 November, 202

Learning goals achieved:

1. I am discovering, exploring and refining my gross and fine motor skills.
2. I am demonstrating positivity in my own abilities.
3. I enjoy listening to and respond to a variety of types of music, sing songs and make music using instruments.

Dispositions/Schemas

3 — ADD THE INTEREST TO THE EMERGENT PLAN

Create new Curriculum Plan

Relationships, words, communication (C, IB)

★ Movement and dance

Sensory materials (Wb, ET, C)

★ Listening to classical music in background in afternoon.

Opportunities to develop large motor skills (Wb, ET)

★ Musical chairs/Hopping Bunnies games

Children's emerging interests/voice

Type here...

Learn opportunities to dance in music games ✕

PROGRESSING CHILD INTEREST

This documentation sequence demonstrates how the educator seamlessly carries the child's interest through the documentation process to support learning:

1. **Notices** the child's interest (notes this on anecdotal note);
2. Continues to observe and **documents a learning story** about a dancing activity (learning story including learning episode, learning achieved and a plan for progression);
3. Includes the child's interest and progressive activities in the forthcoming **emergent plan** (star marks where activities relate to Lewis).

1. Listen-in and observe

The phase of the planning cycle is about listening-in to the child, noticing what they do and collecting information on their interests, preferences, abilities and needs. Information can be gathered by educators making anecdotal notes, short videos or plotting information on a wall chart or notice board.

Listening-in

Taking the time to stand back, listen-in and observe is central to documentation that will support further learning.

Pedagogical strategies include:

- Carrying out **spontaneous or planned observations** and recording informal anecdotal notes (a snapshot of a child at a particular time) can be used to capture interests, dispositions and patterns in play. These can be used to inform curriculum planning or as a learning story.
- Engaging with children in conversation is one of the most **insightful ways** of gathering information about their thoughts, interests and experiences. The early childhood educator records children's comments, using these to analyse children's understanding and to plan the next steps in learning.
- Helping children to think about and reflect on their own learning through self-assessment. By **revisiting** activities, events and interactions, children can **recall** and make **connections** with their prior learning and **reimagine** new learning. Self-assessment gives the early childhood educator insight into areas such as the child's self-esteem, motivation, understanding and perception of themselves as a learner.

2. Document and analyse

Documentation of the process of learning can then be captured using a variety of methods. This includes learning stories, photographs or photographic sequences with child or educator captions, or videos collected in a portfolio. In addition, Living Wall displays, group stories or floor books can be used. These also allow the child, the early childhood educator and family to **revisit, recall and reimagine** learning experiences.

Documentation that is individual to the child (an individual learning story) should be rich and meaningful; it should reflect the learning process, the child's character and abilities. Sharing information with colleagues and family is essential to find out about children at different times and in other places by way of consolidating and affirming learning.

The educator then analyses the information gathered to draw insight and understanding of children's play patterns and learning. The educator draws upon the goals of the curriculum framework to assess learning achievements. During this process the educator can ask themselves:

- What have I observed? (The story of learning)

- What is this telling me? (Dispositions, skills, attitudes, knowledge, understanding)

- How can I build on the child's learning and scaffold this to the next level? (Planning)

3. Plan and implement

Once the educator has analysed the observations gathered through documentation, the way forward is made visible through a documented plan for learning. The plan includes experiences, language, resources, interactions and environments that build on children's interests, preferences, abilities and needs. The aims and goals of the early childhood curriculum framework will provide a holistic structure for this plan.

It is important to highlight that in implementing the curriculum plan, educators **should not over-focus on learning goals**. Certainly, the educator needs to be aware of curriculum themes, aims and goals, however an over-reliance on featuring these on planning documentation **undermines the emergent approach.** Instead ensure the planning framework is **sufficiently broad** to incorporate all the **main themes** of the curriculum framework.

Instead, **take a lead from the child**, allowing for sustained exploration in the child's own time and analysing what's happening on a deeper level **rather than letting prescriptive goals sway or overpower the child's own pathway to learning.**

Every interaction with a child doesn't have to be a '**teachable moment'** that aligns to a learning goal. It is important **not to 'bend' children's play** or interactions to suit a goals led agenda. Instead, listen-in and observe for opportunities that occur naturally as part of play. The educator can then offer suggestions, ask open ended questions and extend naturally occurring interactions and learning. Good-quality child-led learning will involve as many small interactions as big teachable projects.

The interests and needs of individual children as appropriate should be visible on the plan to ensure it is child-inspired. Plans can also draw upon pedagogical strategies that work well with certain children, for example, celebration clapping with a baby; social praise for a toddler or awarding the young child helper status. The plan may also feature children's preferred learning contexts such as outdoors, through movement, alone or in groups.

Implementing the planning cycle involves educators putting their plans into action. Planned and unplanned activities are seamlessly woven into daily interactions, routines and child choices. This includes the indoor and outdoor environment, group projects, free play and investigations.

Plans should be visible in the room where notes can be added and act as a guide for the educator team.

4. Reflect and evaluate

The final stage of the planning cycle is about reflecting on the effectiveness of the plan itself and the process undertaken.

- For example, educators may reflect on some of the following questions:

- How did children respond to activities - what was their level of interest?

- Where suitable resources are available to implement the plan – if not, what is needed for next time?

- Were all children able to participate equally or do changes need to be made?

- Did any new interests reveal themselves and how is this informing documentation?

- Did any spontaneous learning happen that wasn't planned for? Does this require a response?

- Was the planning cycle itself effective for the group or does this need to be modified?

Educators should include children insofar as possible in the reflection process. Take time to listen to children's views about the activities and what they thought of them.

Documenting an Emergent plan

Programme plans inspired by emergent curriculum take many forms. Educators can use a curriculum web plan as a visual account of the learning experiences that are offered across all areas stemming from the combined children and educator interests. A topic scaffold supports the delivery of the plan.

'Topic scaffolds' or themes are a range of interesting subjects used as a vehicle to deliver a broad based curriculum in collaboration with children's interests and needs. Topics can be on any area (Pets, Animals, Clothes, Farm, Things that shine, Senses, and so on). The importance is the appropriateness of the topic to children in the group.

Questions to ask before committing to a topic scaffold/ theme include:

- Can children's emerging interests and needs can be **easily integrated** to the topic/theme?
- Will the topic/theme lend itself to **all curriculum learning themes**?
- Is the topic **meaningful to the lived experience/age/abilities** of children in the group?

- Are all the **resources** that are needed for implementation on hand or can be accessed?

Planning themes that do not connect to the lived experiences of babies, toddlers and young children have their limitations. For example, a toddler working on a **transporting schema** needs the educator to provide the resources to move objects from one place to another, using different trucks, prams, bags, trolleys, trailers and so on.

This child needs the sensory experience of filling and emptying buckets and containers, moving things around and putting things into their pockets. Of little use would be an off the shelf curriculum plan on modes of 'transport' with coordinated aeroplane colouring sheets.

Experiences in each of the curriculum areas are then recorded to reflect these interests. Curriculum headings on a plan may vary according to the age group educators are planning for or reflect individual learning goals or priorities. For example a plan for babies and toddlers may include a broad heading for schemas and secure relationships which are paramount for very young children.

The benefit of the curriculum web is that it allows flexibility in programme delivery in consideration of children's changing needs and interests. It also encourages creative and open-ended shared thinking, which serves as a stark contrast to the restricted, linear approach that is typical of more traditional theme-based planning.

The web plan on the next page blends the topic scaffold of 'Life Cycles' with children's interests and needs on one plan. The plan is framed around broad holistic learning themes.

MOSAIC — Continuous Emergent Plan

Digital Solutions for Early Education

AVRIL MCMONAGLE

Songs/rhymes/music: Sleeping bunnies, Speckled Frog, Chick, chick, chicken, Easter Bunny Dance and Freeze

1. Communicating, words, discussions (C, IB)

Books: Life cycle books. When will I grow up. The Egg Hunt. A little frog in a big pond. Chicken Licken. Shark in the Park.

Discussion and words:
Life cycles - chick, rabbits, Frog, flowers. Hatch burrow, hutch Frogspawn, tadpole, bulbs, oval

7. Outings, visitors or highlights
(Wb, IB, C, ET)

Rachel will be our visiting Shark expert this week. She will tell children about her visit to the aquarium and share pictures of the sharks and dolphins she will read Shark in the Park.

Bunny Picnic - with bunny ears, bobtails and krispie buns!

6. Changes to outdoor environment
(Wb, IB, C, ET)

Decorate on Easter Tree/bush
Outdoor slime pond (bath)
Bunny Hop obstacle dance to music
Bunny picnic
Shark chase game. Swimming shark game

5. Events/Celebrations/Projects
(Wb, IB, C, ET)

Easter art observation activity - cuddly chick/ Easter egg/vase of flowers. Decorate an Easter branch indoors - ribbons, fabric, creative artwork.
Continue to water and weed close spring tulips outdoors.
Its Rachel's birthday on Monday and Tom's birthday on Friday!

Notes/reflections

A great start to our topic plan this week. We talked with the children at the beginning of the week about all the activities planned and we got a few extra suggestions thrown in - sharks being the main one! The different sized cardboard boxes in the loose parts area was a huge hit with children - this led to many rich discussions on different types of homes for animals and people. Children could relate to life cycles really well -many comparing to babies, children and adults. Our decorated Easter tree at the entrance to the setting is a big hit - children bring things from home and its filling up nicely. Our Easter Tuff Tray didn't draw much interest - we are changing materials for the coming week. We are extending the overall theme into next week as there is still lots to do and discover. Some new emerging interests will be incorporated based on observations and discussions and we plan to change some of the indoor resources. 14.22.

CHILDREN'S EMERGING INTERESTS AND VOICE

Messy play
Sand
Paint
Cooking fun
Using and making objects
Picking flowers
Outside and running
Making books
Dressing up

2. Real materials/loose parts
(ET, C, Wb)

Loose Parts. different sized boxes to make houses, corks, bottle tops and small wooden sticks. Cooked and uncooked egg shells and float. Painting eggs and stones
Paint and decorate an Easter branch.
Natural objects for lining up positioning indoors and outdoors

3. Changes to indoor environment

Add life cycle provocations all around the room as discussion points. Arrange tapioca frog spawn use life cycle puzzles for discussion
Provide cardboard and craft materials to make bunny ears and bobtails, Easter eggs etc.
Role play Easter shop selling Easter themed items, cards Easter Tuff Tray, ice cube melt frozen flowers.

4. Research and finding out about things
(Wb, IB, ET, C)

Find out about life cycles on the computer. Find and print images of various stages, discuss what's interesting some, different.

Find out about Easter - what does it mean?.

Life Cycles & Children's Interests

Support for individual emerging interests/needs:

Child: *Support me to practise:*

SG: support to lengthen sentences

TC: practice gross motor skills and spatial perception outdoors

RT: positive reinforcement for short periods of concentration and focus

BC: encourage to experience messy play

HJ: encourage to speak during quiet li time with KW

SMcF: support behaviour targets from Snapshot Review.

Date from: 4th April to 8th April 2022.

www.mosaicearlyed.com

*This succinct piece of documented evidence of learning skilfully reveals that learning is happening holistically and seamlessly as a small group of children work together to solve a problem. It clearly demonstrates the competent and confident decision making of the children involved in this lovely play episode. The educator provided the **'invitation to play'** and the children did the rest!*

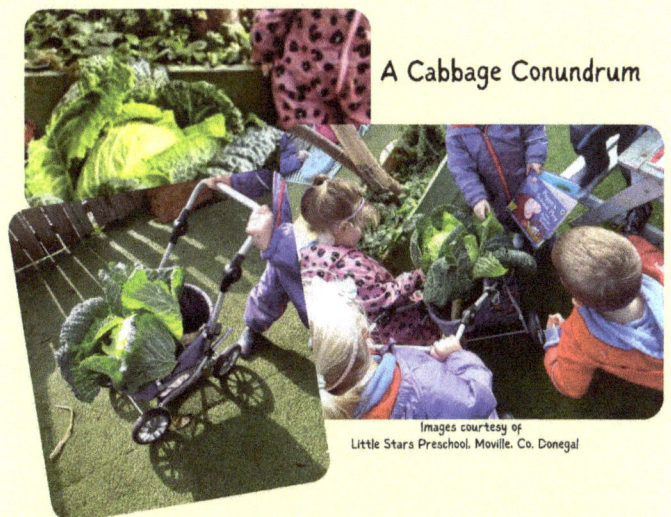

A Cabbage Conundrum

Images courtesy of
Little Stars Preschool, Moville, Co. Donegal

We faced a huge **cabbage shaped dilemma** today. We needed to bring our cabbages inside from the garden but they were too heavy to carry.

We **collaborated** to find a solution.
We put forward different **ideas** about how we could carry the cabbages.
We **listened** to each others ideas.
We **tested** different **theories** and **suggestions.**

We looked around for things that could transport the cabbages.
The sand lorry? We **observed** that it was too small. The shopping bag? We **decided** that it might get squished. The hula hoop? On **investigating** the size of the hula hoop, we **determined** that the cabbages might fall through.

We **identified** a practical **solution** which was right beside us all the time. We **calculated** that it would be best to transport our precious cargo **one at a time.**

How did the cabbage conundrum progress?

The Cabbage Conundrum didn't stop there. It opened up a range of **continued explorations, discussions and learning possibilities**.

Educators and children printed photographs of the cabbage conundrum and placed them in the poly tunnel. The images will not only spark discussion and reflection, but they also demonstrate the finished product when next year's seeds are planted.

This prompted questions about vegetables in general and a whole range of additional explorations and learning opportunities. A **Living Wall** display called *'What we know about fruit and vegetables'* was a progressive project where children's thoughts and comments were added over time.

Images courtesy of the outdoor classroom at Little Stars Pre-School, Moville, Co. Donegal

A SUITCASE FULL OF STORIES

This emergent plan created on MOSAIC Educator (here and on next page), demonstrates a continuation of the Cabbage Conundrum. The activity and general growing activities in the preschool have led to the development of an emergent plan called 'Fruit and Vegetables with Children's Interests'.

Note the lightbulb symbol beside certain activities. This reminds educators that this is linked to a child's unique interest and ensures the interest isn't lost in the bigger topic.

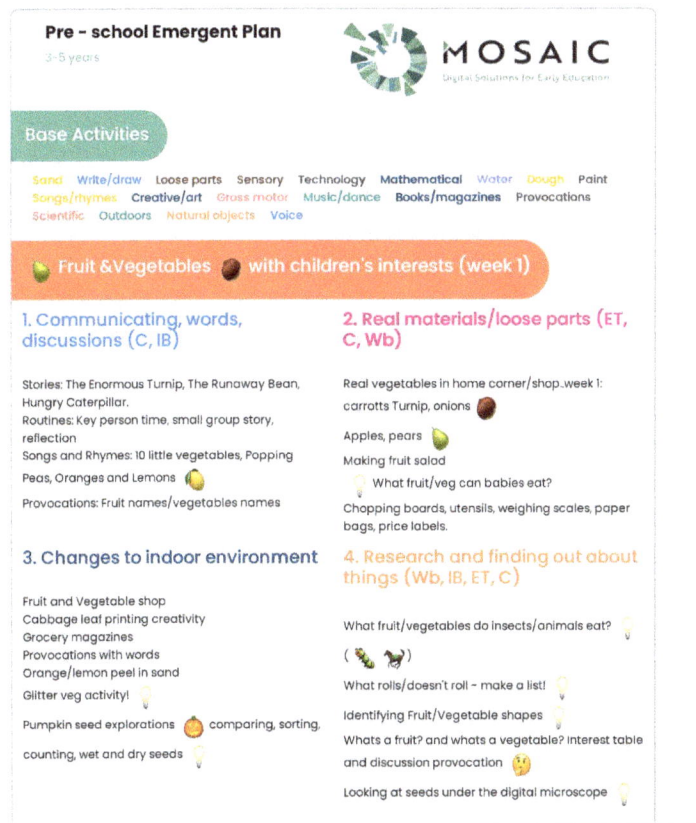

Activities are framed around curriculum themes (Aistear), the topic scaffold (Fruit and Vegetables) and children's unique interests. All are blended together on one flexible emergent plan that will evolve over the weeks ahead.

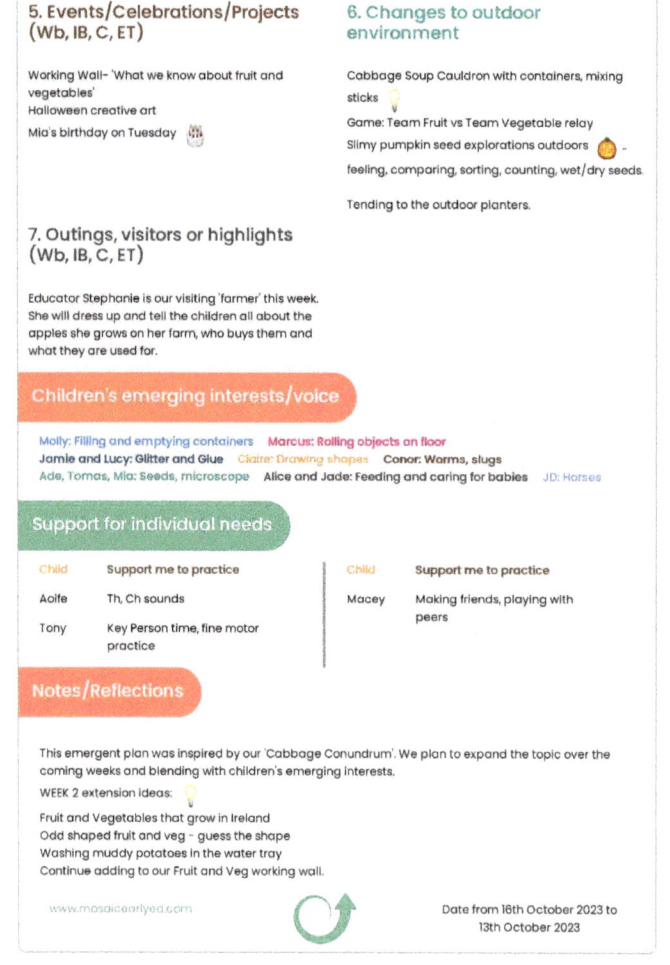

5. Events/Celebrations/Projects (Wb, IB, C, ET)

Working Wall- 'What we know about fruit and vegetables'
Halloween creative art
Mia's birthday on Tuesday 🎂

6. Changes to outdoor environment

Cabbage Soup Cauldron with containers, mixing sticks 💡
Game: Team Fruit vs Team Vegetable relay
Slimy pumpkin seed explorations outdoors 🎃 - feeling, comparing, sorting, counting, wet/dry seeds.
Tending to the outdoor planters.

7. Outings, visitors or highlights (Wb, IB, C, ET)

Educator Stephanie is our visiting 'farmer' this week. She will dress up and tell the children all about the apples she grows on her farm, who buys them and what they are used for.

Children's emerging interests/voice

Molly: Filling and emptying containers   Marcus: Rolling objects on floor
Jamie and Lucy: Glitter and Glue   Claire: Drawing shapes   Conor: Worms, slugs
Ade, Tomas, Mia: Seeds, microscope   Alice and Jade: Feeding and caring for babies   JD: Horses

Support for individual needs

Child	Support me to practice	Child	Support me to practice
Aoife	Th, Ch sounds	Macey	Making friends, playing with peers
Tony	Key Person time, fine motor practice		

Notes/Reflections

This emergent plan was inspired by our 'Cabbage Conundrum'. We plan to expand the topic over the coming weeks and blending with children's emerging interests.

WEEK 2 extension ideas: 💡

Fruit and Vegetables that grow in Ireland
Odd shaped fruit and veg - guess the shape
Washing muddy potatoes in the water tray
Continue adding to our Fruit and Veg working wall.

www.mosaicearlyed.com

Date from 16th October 2023 to 13th October 2023

Digital Emergent Planning

Digital emergent planning offers many time saving advantages to the educator. Plans can be **created, saved and edited** on an ongoing basis in response to children's emerging interests.

For example, the digital plan on MOSAIC Educator has several key components in line with good pedagogical practice.

- **Title of plan,** week number, date and time frame . Activities are framed around a topic scaffold yet incorporate children's emerging interests and needs seamlessly under one flexible plan that includes a range of individual and small group activities.

- **Base activities.** The inclusion of base activities in the plan enables the educator to prioritise the resources needed to implement the plan.

- **Holistic headings** incorporating curriculum themes (these match the curriculum statement for the early childhood setting).

- **Children's observed or communicated interests.** A lightbulb symbol is added where the activity is directly linked to an emerging interest.

- **Any specific supports/differentiation** for individual children. This information will enable all educators to support children's individual needs and stage of development in a time sensitive manner.

- **Reflection/evaluation** enables educators to reflect on engagement and the planning process itself.

Listening in and observing children's engagement with planned and spontaneous play activities, will provide rich and meaningful information for learning stories and documented learning scenarios.

> *The emergent plan called 'Healthy Hearts' was created on MOSAIC Educator (next page). This piece of documentation demonstrates the skill of the educator in creating a plan using the topic scaffold of Healthy Hearts. This will bring meaning to the Valentine's Day celebration whilst incorporating interests and new learning in a way that children can connect with.*

A SUITCASE FULL OF STORIES

Pre - school Emergent Plan
3-5 years

Base Activities

Write/draw Loose parts Sensory **Technology** Drama Water Dough Paint Songs/rhymes
Special interest Creative/art Gross motor Music/dance Imaginative/role Provocations
Scientific Outdoors Natural objects Self-care/well-being Voice

💓 Healthy Hearts with Children's Interests 💛 (Wk 1)

1. Communicating, words, discussions (C, IB)

 Songs/Rhymes.. I love you, 5 Little Valentines, You are my Sunshine
Words/Discussion.. heart, love, hug, friendship, care, empathy, kindness, feelings, emotions, magic potion ingredients list, a healthy heart, body parts.
Stories/Books: My Body, Love you to the Moon, Mamma Bear hugs

2. Real materials/loose parts (ET, C, Wb)

 Loose Part collage for children's interpretation of the heart shape.. buttons, bottle tops, shiny paper, petals; card, paper;
 Old valentine cards for cut and stick;
 Containers to transport loose parts to different activities;
 Make special junk gifts for the gift shop

3. Changes to indoor environment

 Provocations: Role play flower and gift shop;
Heart shapes and balloons;
Body Chart showing organs;
 Group activity: make a heart garland to decorate the room;
Caring words speech bubbles on windows/walls;
Fizzy hearts experiment using bath bombs.

4. Research and finding out about things (Wb, IB, ET, C)

Create a large heart map for the wall. Encourage children to contribute to the map by adding a picture of someone they love, a favourite place or object.
 Support children to use technology to photograph their work.
 Doctors heart check
Find out about a real heart - what is it for? ...where is it in our body?... what does it look like? How can we keep our heart healthy? What does it sound like?

5. Events/Celebrations/Projects (Wb, IB, C, ET)

Valentines Day creativity

Joanne's birthday on Tuesday

'What we know about our Heart' Working Wall project - children's voice/photography.

6. Changes to outdoor environment

Hanging hearts from junk art for trees and fence outside;

Make a magic love potion outside using natural things like petals;

Running, skipping, hopping for a healthy heart - feel/listen to your heart after exercise.

 Treasure hunt for heart shaped stones and leaves - count shape, size texture chart.

7. Outings, visitors or highlights (Wb, IB, C, ET)

 Rachel will be our 'Travelling Magician' this week. She will dress up to perform magic tricks and help children devise an ingredients list for the magic love potion we will make outside.

Maggie will be our visiting 'Doctor' in her white coat. She will talk about keeping our heart healthy. We will listen to our heart through a stethoscope.

Children's emerging interests/voice

CARLA: magic tricks   MARC: playing shop   MACEY: taking photos   MARION: playing doctor
MATTHEW, LISA, JON: transporting schema   TONI: cutting out with real scissors!
ASHA: glue and sticking pictures   THOMAS: flowers   MAY: Singing   Tomas: Pirate treasure

Support for individual needs

Child	Support me to practice	Child	Support me to practice
CJ	Confidence outdoors	Macey	Focus and concentration
Tony	Fine motor		

Notes/Reflections

We decided to use the upcoming Valentine's Day celebration as a support for a topic on the heart. The children were talking about seeing heart symbols in their environment. We plan to use this prompt to delve deeper into learning about the human heart. This will give us lots of opportunities to explore personal well-being including physical health and excercise. Children's emerging interests and needs are blended into the plan. When brainstorming the types of things we would do in this topic, the children came up with some interesting ideas - in particular getting a stethoscope to listen to hearts!

We will alter the plan next week depending on engagement and experiences this week

Things to remember about emergent planning

- Topic scaffolds/themes must have meaning to the age group being planned for. Is the topic scaffold something that is part of the **child's lived experience**, can they **identify** with it?

- Using what you already know about children, brainstorm potential learning opportunities based on **emerging interests**.

- The plan should incorporate **continuation and progression** in learning - can you **connect and build** on earlier learning?

- The plan is open and continuous and is updated **weekly/fortnightly** by the team.

- Anecdotal notes are collected on an **ongoing basis**.

- Educators do not have to start from scratch each week. Simply add/change areas of the plan to let it **flow to reflect the changing interests of children** and how responses have been provided with different materials or prompts.

- Only note **changes** to the indoor/outdoor environment – e.g. home corner to hospital, new books or props. Include resources or loose parts to be included to help implement the plan. Base activities listed will support this.

- The plan must be **sufficiently broad and equitable** to meet the needs of all children whilst having a sufficient focus on learning and development.

Things to remember about planning for babies and toddlers

- Planning for the under 3's is fluid, flexible and ongoing. Babies/toddlers need opportunities for lots of repetition. **Do not rush** experiences or areas being explored.

- **Listen-in and observe the voice** of babies and toddlers - note their gestures, facial expressions, vocalisations and play patterns.

- Observe **schemas** and emerging development and use them to inform planned activities.

- Things like throwing a ball, crawling and saying words are an **'interest'** or the child is working on a schema like 'trajectory'.

- The more **open-ended** materials available, the more natural interests you will stimulate and observe.

- Simple **'serve and return'** games with babies and toddlers should be a part of daily interactions and planned activities to build relationships.

This emergent plan created on MOSAIC Educator for children under 3 years (on next 2 pages), has an additional focus on schemas, well-being, security and belonging and sensory development in line with for baby and toddler development.

The pre-school plan and the under 3's plan can be used interchangeably or as deemed suitable for the children in the group.

A SUITCASE FULL OF STORIES

Under 3's Emergent Plan
0-3 years

Base Activities

Sand   Mark making   Loose parts   Sensory   Technology   Drama   Water   Dough   Paint
Songs/rhymes   Creative/art   Manipulative   Gross motor   Music/dance   Books/magazines
Outdoors   Natural objects   Self-care/well-being   Rest/quiet   Voice

 Stories & Rhymes with Children's Interests (Wk 3&4: Sheep)

1. Well-being, security / belonging (Wb, IB)

Continuing to talk about favourite comfort objects/cuddly toys;
Variety of sheep toys and stuffed animals- children bring in their own;

 Hand puppet and peek a boo interactions;

Singing rhymes during care routines using facial expression and exaggerated gestures;

 Using soothing music for sleep time.

2. Relationships, words, communication (C, IB)

Songs/rhymes: Ba Ba Black Sheep; Mary had a little lamb; Little Bo Peep;
Rhyming patterns during care routines;
Words: Soft, fluffy, cosy, warm, lamb, sheep;
Stories: Sheep in a Jeep, Where is the green sheep?

3. Sensory materials (Wb, ET, C)

Sensory boxes full of tactile fabrics - fake fur, wool, cotton wool, balls of wool;
Guess the animal sound recordings;

 Shadows using torches and lights on wall;

Small animal figures in jelly on play trays;
Outdoor exploring- finding animals in the sandbox.

4. Opportunities to develop small motor skills (Wb, ET)

 Old McDonald finger puppets;

Collage pictures using assorted fabric pieces;
Feeding sheep floor tuff tray using rice krispies;
Squeezing cotton wool in water bowls.

5. Opportunities to support schemas (Wb, IB, C, ET)

Transporting: small animal figures and trucks, bags and baskets;
Positioning: loose part natural objects and small figures in baskets;
Trajectory: throwing small bean bags into baskets game.

6. Events/Celebrations/Projects (Wb, IB, C, ET)

Aoife's birthday on Wednesday, Patrick's birthday on Thursday

Birthday dancing to music

7. Opportunities to develop large motor skills (Wb, ET)

The sheep are in the meadow floor game;

 Outdoor sheep treasure hunt- We are all going on a sheep hunt – up hill and down hill;

 Dancing sheep musical game.

Children's emerging interests/voice

Molly and Patrick: Transporting schema   Alice: Climbing   Tomas and Carrie: Positioning schema
Soirse: Music   Artem: Outdoor explorations   Alise and Rory: Puppets   CJ: Torches and light

Support for individual needs

Child	Support me to practice	Child	Support me to practice
Aoife	Settling in morning	Freddie	Balance and nagivating space

Notes/Reflections

We are continuing our topic scaffold of stories and nursery rhymes. Over the past 2 weeks our focus on bears 🧸 provided multiple learning opportunities and fun. The Teddy Bear pram race and the picnic outdoors was the highlight for toddlers! The resources the team could use to support the bear theme were plentiful and the topic will merge into the forthcoming weeks activities. We have decided to extend using sheep 🐑 as a focus this week and next as this will give us lots of new resources, songs, words and stories. We are continuing to incorporate emerging schemas and observed interests into daily activities so that children can revisit and progress their skills and interests. Pictures of our stories and rhymes topic scaffold are displayed at low level on the toddler room walls for revisiting and reflection.

In this under 3's example (on next 2 pages), a topic scaffold of 'Senses' is used to frame baby and toddler interests, preferences, abilities and needs. Again, note the connection between the child's interest and a planned activity.

Note the broad plan headings which are holistic in nature and incorporate curriculum themes.

A SUITCASE FULL OF STORIES

Under 3's Emergent Plan
0-3 years

Base Activities

Sand   Mark making   Loose parts   Sensory   Water   Dough   Foam   Paint   Puzzles/games
Songs/rhymes   Special interest   Creative/art   Manipulative   Gross motor   Music/dance
Outdoors   Natural objects   Self-care/well-being   Rest/quiet

🌻 Senses with Children's Interests (Week 2)

1. Well-being, security / belonging (Wb, IB)

Welcome song in the morning- each child named;
Interaction and playful songs during feeding/changing;
1:1 Key person time
;
Serve and Return interactions.

2. Relationships, words, communication (C, IB)

Songs and Rhymes – I see you, I am special because, Mirror, Mirror.
Stories: Johnny can Taste, Smell, See and Hear, Who is in the mirror? The Hungry Caterpillar.

 Peek a boo games;

New words: Senses words- hard, soft, squishy etc.; rotation words- round, circle, spin; reflection/mirror, light/dark/, bitter/sweet.

3. Sensory materials (Wb, ET, C)

Sensory dough/foam- lemon/mint;
Mirrors and lights;
 Water sponges and water wheel;
Orange and lemon peel in sand;
Add coloured lights to the Sensory Tent this week.

4. Opportunities to develop small motor skills (Wb, ET)

Coloured pasta;
Natural loose parts- shells, stones, dried seaweed
Feeding utensils;
Manipulating moon dough;
Squeezing sponges in water.

5. Opportunities to support schemas (Wb, IB, C, ET)

 Filling and emptying different sized containers;

 Soft climbing obstacle course;

Spinning windmills/ discs outdoors;

Wrapping resources - scarves, blankets, paper

6. Events/Celebrations/Projects (Wb, IB, C, ET)

Exploring senses;
Rachel's birthday is on Wednesday
Patrick's baby sister comes home on Friday

7. Opportunities to develop large motor skills (Wb, ET)

 Musical floor games;

 Dancing to music;

 Wallpaper on floor for mark making;

 Throwing balls into tubs floor game;

 Sensory snow foam in bun trays.

Children's emerging interests/voice

Caroline: enveloping schema   Cormac: spinning objects   Eoghain: moving to music
Erin: crawling and exploring   Eabha, Ryan, Grace: foam, bubbles
Saoirse, Caitlin, Oran: Peek a boo games   Culann: emptying and filling

Support for individual needs

Child	Support me to practice	Child	Support me to practice
Aoife	Reassurance after nap	Sarah	Playing outside

Notes/Reflections

Now on week 2, the senses topic is lending itself to a lot of spontaneous activities and its interesting to watch the babies and wobblers explore new different smells, tastes and sounds.

Most obvious this week was the children's reaction to the sensory tent! A number of children spontaneously crawled inside and just spent time looking at the lights – a few even fell asleep.

We hung spinning discs in the classroom windows and brought them outdoors too – this led to interest in reflections and bright colours! We did a shout out to parents to bring in old discs and we now are going to plan further activities with these.

There is plenty more to explore with the senses topic so we are going to keep going by changing up some of the resources and see what interests emerge from this next week!

www.mosaicearlyed.com

Date from 18th September 2023 to 13th October 2023

CHAPTER 10
Packing the Suitcase

Going back to where we began - packing the invisible suitcase.

Below are some key considerations and messages that will lead to the creation of a balanced invisible suitcase for all children:

- Whilst a child may not have the power to change life circumstances, supportive relationships and validation from significant adults will go a long way in affording them the emotional security to thrive and learn.

- A one size fits all approach to early education neglects the individuality of the child. Educators must be able to see and respond to the child's uniqueness - their social circumstances, strengths, preferences and neurodiversity.

- Giving children time is vital in early education. Time to experience, time to revisit, time to recall and time to reimagine. Above all else educators and early education stakeholders must be advocates for time.

- The role of the proficient educator is central to effective early education. The ability of an educator to interact, understand and respond to a child is the key determining factor for positive well-being and learning outcomes.

- Pedagogical documentation is one of the most insightful and effective teaching and learning strategies that educators have at their disposal. It deserves recognition as such and should not be seen as an optional extra.

- The Learning Story Approach is the key to authentic child-centred assessment for learning that is easily married with a child-inspired curriculum for all children.

- The most important verbs in early education are not 'to talk' 'to teach' or 'to show' – but to 'listen-in'. This practice is not confined to children who have spoken language. Children of all ages and abilities show us their interests, preferences and needs through play and behaviour.

- Emergent curriculum does not magically happen. It requires that educators actively seek out and plan for the interests and needs of the individual child. An ongoing cycle of documentation greatly informs and supports this process.

- When planning learning experiences for babies, toddlers and young children, ensuring that activities have meaning and are reflective of lived experience is vital. Providing experiences in a way that doesn't reflect the landscape of children's lived experience is futile.

- Digital documentation offers many advantages. Its multi-modality offers a more connective and shareable form of documentation which is accessible to family in real time creating opportunities for discussion, reflection and consolidation with children at home.

- The principles of rights-based, child-led early education as the most fundamental stage of education must be upheld. 'It is easier to build strong children than to repair broken people'.

References

Aistear The Early Childhood Curriculum Framework (2009) National Council for Curriculum and Assessment. Ireland.

Bezemer, Jeff, and Gunther Kress. (2016). Multimodality, Learning and Communication: A Social Semiotic Frame. London: Routledge, Taylor & Francis Group

Carr, M. (2001) Assessment in early childhood settings: Learning stories. London: Paul Chapman Publishing.

Carr M, Cowie B and Mitchell L (2016) Documentation in Early Childhood Research: Practice and Research Informing Each Other. In: Farrell A, Kagan S and Tisdall K (eds) The SAGE Handbook of Early Childhood Research. London: SAGE, pp. 277–291.

Carlsen, K. & Clark A. (2022) Potentialities of pedagogical documentation as an intertwined research process with children and teachers in slow pedagogies, European Early Childhood Education Research Journal, 30:2, 200-212, DOI: 10.1080/1350293X.2022.2046838

Clark, A. (2017) Listening to Young Children (expanded 3rd Edition): The Mosaic Approach. Jessica Kingsley Publishers. UK.

Clark, A. 2020. "Towards a Listening ECEC System: Valuing Slow Pedagogy and Slow Knowledge." In Transforming Early Childhood in England, edited by P. Moss and C. Cameron, 134–150. London: UCL Press.

Cook, T., and E. Hess. 2007. "What the Camera Sees and from Whose Perspective: Fun Methodologies for Engaging Children and Enlightening Adults." Childhood 14 (1): 29–45.

Cowan, K. & Flewitt, R. (2021): Moving from paper-based to digital documentation in Early Childhood Education: democratic potentials and challenges, International Journal of Early Years Education, DOI: 10.1080/09669760.2021.2013171

Cowie, B., and Carr, M. (2004) The consequences of socio-cultural assessment. In A. Anning, J. Cullen and M. Fleer (Eds.) Early Childhood Education: Society and Culture. London: Sage Publications.

Dahlberg, G., P. Moss and A. Pence (2007), Beyond Quality in Early Childhood Education and Care: Languages of Evaluation, 2nd ed., Falmer Press, London.

Formosinho, Julia, and Christine Pascal. 2017. Assessment and Evaluation for Transformation in Early Childhood. 1st ed. London: Routledge

Gardner, H. Multiple Intelligences as a Partner in School Improvement. Educational Leadership, September 1997, 55(1), pp. 20-21.

Giudici, C., C. Rinaldi and M. Krechevsky, eds. (2001), Making Learning Visible: Children as Individual and Group Learners, Project Zero and Reggio Children, Cambridge, Mass. and Reggio Emilia.

Goleman. D. (1995) Emotional Intelligence: Why it can matter more than IQ. Bloomsbury. London.

Lundy. L. (2007) in Participation Framework National Framework for Children and Young People's Participation in Decision-making (2021), Department of Children, Equality, Disability, Integration and Youth. Government of Ireland.

Malaguzzi, L. (1996). The Hundred Languages of Children: The Reggio Emilia Approach to Early Childhood Education. New Jersey: Ablex Publishing Corporation.

Ministry of Education (2017) Te Whāriki. Wellington, New Zealand: New Zealand Government. Available at: https://www.education.govt.nz/early-childhood/teaching-and-learning/te-whariki/ (accessed 12 January 2023).

United Nations (UN) (1989) United Nations Convention on the Rights of the Child, Geneva: Office of the High Commissioner for Human Rights.

Vygotsky, L. S. (1978). Mind in society: The development of higher psychological processes. (Edited by M. Cole, J. Scribner, V. John-Steiner, & E. Souberman). Cambridge, MA: Harvard University Press.

Find out more about the Mosaic system

MOSAIC Digital Solutions of Early Education, a company inspired by the vision and passion of founder Avril McMonagle, has a simple yet powerful mission: To revolutionise early childcare education through innovative technology. With Avril haven worked in early childhood education for over 30 years, she understands the challenges faced by educators in compiling and sharing important portfolios with parents, which is why she created two key products - MOSAIC Educator and MOSAIC Family apps.

The unique value of these apps lies in providing a green, secure alternative to traditional paper-based portfolios while meeting legal requirements and quality standards in early education. The cloud-based electronic storybooks offer real-time updates on each child's progress, including photos, videos, learning stories, and reports that parents can access through the MOSAIC Family app.

This empowers both educators and families with an efficient communication platform that actively involves them in their child's learning journey. Their customers have seen first-hand how this has enriched their experience resulting in an ever growing market share across Ireland and setting their sights further afield where they envision expanding into new international markets where their technology can make an even bigger impact on early childhood education, reach a larger demographic and municipal educational systems.

Find out more about the range of services Avril and the MOSAIC team offers by visiting their website: **https://mosaicearlyed.com/**

For sponsorship/funding queries, please contact Avril directly on **avrilmosaic1@gmail.com**

www.ingramcontent.com/pod-product-compliance
Lightning Source LLC
Chambersburg PA
CBHW041312110526
44591CB00022B/2889